D0909907

THE POWER
OF PROTEST

*A National Study
of Student and Faculty Disruptions
with Implications for the Future*

Alexander W. Astin
Helen S. Astin
Alan E. Bayer
Ann S. Bisconti

THE POWER

OF PROTEST

Jossey-Bass Publishers
San Francisco • Washington • London • 1975

THE POWER OF PROTEST

A National Study of Student and Faculty Disruptions with Implications for the Future
    by Alexander W. Astin, Helen S. Astin, Alan E. Bayer, Ann S. Bisconti

45,608

The Jossey-Bass
Series in Higher Education

PREFACE

The idea for a national study of campus unrest and change originated in a seminar on the college environment held at the Center for Advanced Study in the Behavioral Sciences (Stanford, California) during the 1967–1968 academic year. Several of the attending fellows had more than an academic interest in campus unrest. One was forced to return to his campus because his laboratory had been shut by protesters who chained themselves to the doors. The university of another was closed after a violent confrontation between police and students in which injuries and arrests occurred. Many of the other fellows were on leave from campuses that had also been severely disrupted by protests. It is hardly surprising, then, that the topic of campus unrest was of central interest. Indeed, an entire series of seminar meetings was devoted to discussions between the fellows and selected college and university presidents who had been invited to the center to speak about their experiences with campus unrest.

The fellows participating in the seminar became sufficiently convinced of the need for a systematic and comprehensive study of campus unrest to draft a statement that was eventually published in *Science* (July 5, 1968, p. 23) under the title "Student Protests: A Phenomenon for Behavioral Sciences Research": "It is obvious that this phenomenon is importantly affecting university structure and function. It is also obvious that it is receiving a tremendous amount of attention and reaction. Because of this importance and visibility, it deserves the kind of comprehensive examination that can provide insights into the behavioral aspects of the phenomenon. . . . A national study to examine student unrest, . . . dedicated to a better understanding of the dynamics of the process of student protest, can be useful in resolving the substantive issues which are raised in these protests. . . . The problem is important in its own right as an area for behavioral research."

The prime mover in urging a comprehensive national study was one of the most active seminar participants, Eli A. Rubinstein, on leave from the National Institute of Mental Health (NIMH), where he was assistant director for extramural programs. In the spring of 1968, Rubinstein called together a group of behavioral scientists and college administrators to discuss the possibility of such a study. As a result, the American Council on Education (ACE) was asked in September 1968 to submit a proposal to NIMH, which convened a special review committee in late October. The proposal was favorably reviewed, and the three-year study began officially in December 1968.

The design of the study and the controversy it engendered are described in Chapter One. A basic aim of *The Power of Protest* is to reexamine the findings that emerged from the study, focusing on the relationship between campus unrest and the subsequent changes that have taken place in American higher education. An additional purpose is to make publicly available, for the first time, the major findings of the ACE comprehensive program of research on the topic.

A summary of the highlights of an unrest era (1962–1971) are presented in Chapter Two. The next four chapters present a sequential analysis of the phenomenon of unrest: antecedent factors that determine which campuses will experience protests and which persons are likely to get involved (Chapter Three), the dynamics of protests as revealed through a detailed analysis of individual protest events (Chapters Four and Five), and the outcomes of protest as measured by changes in institutions and individuals (Chapter Six).

The final chapter (Seven) begins with a brief summary of

highlights from the empirical studies, then discusses alternative theories of the decline in campus activism, and concludes with an overview of campus unrest today and an assessment of prospects for the future.

The Power of Protest is intended for a general audience of persons concerned with higher education. College administrators, who were probably among those most significantly affected by campus protests, will be especially interested in why protests often arise in response to administrative decisions and how administrative behavior can affect the course of a protest (Chapters Four and Five).

College faculty members—whatever their discipline—will be interested in the key role played by faculty in initiating and supporting many types of campus protests (see, in particular, Chapters Three, Four, and Five). Faculty members in the social sciences may be interested in the antagonism toward the study evidenced by many of their colleagues (Chapter One) and in possible implications for their own studies of controversial issues.

Finally, the book should be of interest to the general community of social and behavioral scientists, particularly to those interested in research on socially controversial issues (Chapter One). The methodologically inclined social scientist will be interested in the varieties of methods used: multivariate analyses of longitudinal survey data, analysis of population trends over time ("social indicators"), personal interviews, and case studies. A particularly promising method for possible use in future studies is the approach that we developed for quantitative analysis of qualitative phenomena such as newspaper accounts of protest incidents (see Chapter Four and, for more detail, Bisconti and Astin, 1973).

We are indebted to a number of persons who contributed their energies and talents to this complex undertaking. At the Bureau of Social Science Research, where the twenty-two case studies were undertaken, we received substantial assistance from Michele Harway and Richard Hofrichter. At ACE we were assisted in various phases of the project by Barbara A. Blandford, Jeffrey Dutton, Christine Kelley, Melvina Kelly, Terry G. Mahn, Gerald T. Richardson, Jeannie T. Royer, and Joan Trexler. At ACE we are also particularly indebted to Linda Molm, who performed much of the work relating to Chapter Six, and to Laura Kent, who prepared the section in Chapter Two on the history of campus unrest and who also edited most of the manuscript. Margo R. King, formerly at ACE and now at UCLA, typed the entire manuscript.

We are also indebted to the many students, faculty members, and administrators who helped provide data for the project and to the several persons who visited the twenty-two campuses to collect data for the case studies: Sandra T. Bates, Lawrence Dawson, David A. Duty, Stuart Eber, Gretchen Groth, Philip K. Hastings, Ross Hindman, Nancy Hom, James E. Jones, Lawrence G. Jones, Marjorie Lozoff, Frank N. Magid Associates, Harold Mendelsohn, Robert Michielutte, Stephen J. Miller, Lois Moore, Better Parry, Gubbi Sachidanandan, and Benjamin Wright, Jr.

Our advisory committee for the project provided much needed advice, criticism, and support, particularly in the early, tumultuous stages. Its members were Christian Bay, Allan Cartter, Amitai Etzioni, Andrew Greeley, Seymour Halleck, Wayne Holtzman, Joseph Kauffman, Kenneth Keniston, David Riesman, Eli Rubinstein, Brewster Smith, and Preston Valien.

Finally, we express our appreciation to the NIMH for its financial support of the project and especially for its "hands off" attitude toward the conduct of this research.

Los Angeles   ALEXANDER W. ASTIN
September 1975   HELEN S. ASTIN
                                                  ALAN E. BAYER
                                                  ANN S. BISCONTI

CONTENTS

THE POWER
OF PROTEST

*A National Study
of Student and Faculty Disruptions
with Implications for the Future*

I

CONTROVERSIAL STUDY OF CONTROVERSY

The days when newspaper headlines announced one violent student protest after another seem to belong to a far distant past. In the intervening years, we have witnessed the elimination of United States involvement in Vietnam, the funeral of President Johnson, and the resignation of President Nixon, and we have grappled publicly and privately with serious economic problems. College placement offices, once the scene of protests against recruiters representing the "military-industrial enemy," now are filled with anxious students hoping to make a favorable impression on the limited number of recruiters who still make campus calls. It seems that campus unrest faded out as abruptly as it appeared, leaving hardly a trace. In fact, although the incidence of campus unrest has declined, the years of turmoil (1966 to 1971) left much more than a trace. The legacy of campus unrest is far-reaching—from the dramatic changes in stu-

1

dent enrollments, student views, and student life to the revolutionary curriculum approaches much publicized today.

How these changes occurred has not received nearly the attention that was devoted to campus crises during the protest years, and yet a study of the links between the unrest of yesterday and the campus of today is necessary in order to understand how we came so far so fast.

To provide perspectives on the links between the two campus eras and to gain some insight on future directions, we have re-examined the findings of what was probably the most comprehensive study of campus unrest ever undertaken. The program, carried out through the American Council on Education (ACE) with funds from the National Institute of Mental Health, covered a three-year period; component projects included national studies of students and faculty, intensive case studies, and analysis of campus newspaper reports. The study itself became a source of controversy, evoking protests from students, faculty members, and others associated with the academic world.

Design of the Study

The American Council on Education was asked to conduct the study primarily because it had already collected extensive longitudinal data on students and college environments through its Cooperative Institutional Research Program (CIRP) and because its research staff had experience in studying the impact of college on students. Specifically, the three-year project sought to answer the following questions:

What is the frequency and extent of campus unrest in American higher education? How many campuses and how many students are involved? What are present trends in the frequency and severity of protests? What do these trends suggest for the immediate future?

What factors determine whether a student participates in protest, opposes protest, or remains uninvolved? To what extent can a student's protest behavior be predicted from his or her personal characteristics at the time of matriculation?

What environmental factors account for differences among

institutions in the frequency and severity of the protests they experience? How important are such structural factors as size, type of community, and living arrangements? Do administrative practices play an important role, or are protests more or less inevitable, given a particular student clientele? Are there important interactions between administrative practices and student characteristics?

How is the course of a protest affected by the administration's response? Do particular administrative policies either give rise to protest activity or affect the course of a protest once it begins?

How important are student peer groups in affecting protest behavior? What role do the various student organizations play?

How does the faculty affect student unrest? To what extent does faculty encouragement increase the likelihood that student protest will emerge?

What is the role played by various news media, including the student newspaper? Is the course of a demonstration affected by news coverage?

What impact do various types of demonstrations or confrontations have on the college environment? What types of administrative and curricular changes can be attributed to protests? How are the various members of the academic community affected? Are participants and nonparticipants affected differently?

Although the study was to rely heavily on longitudinal data from the ACE, the proposal also provided for a series of intensive case studies of protests on individual campuses. Since ACE did not have sufficient staff for conducting individual interviews in the field, the case studies were subcontracted to the Bureau of Social Science Research (BSSR), a Washington-based research organization.

ACE Research Program. The Cooperative Institutional Research Program (CIRP) at ACE was initiated in the fall of 1966, using a national sample of 246 institutions. It is now carried out under continuing ACE support by the Laboratory for Research on Higher Education at UCLA and includes a sample of some six hundred institutions. The design for selecting institutions (Creager, 1968) was intended to maximize diversity in the sample and to represent all types of higher education institutions.

The general plan is that each fall the entire entering freshman class of a participating institution is surveyed at the time it enters college, usually during the registration or orientation period. The survey instrument, the Student Information Form (SIF), asks for standard biographical and demographic information as well as for information on the student's academic and career plans, life goals, self-concept, attitudes, values, and daily activities. Many of the items on the SIF are the same from year to year, whereas others are added to cover questions of current interest. For instance, the 1966 and 1967 freshmen were asked whether they had participated in demonstrations of any kind while in high school. The 1968 and 1969 freshmen were asked for detailed information about their protest participation—namely, whether they had demonstrated for change in a racial policy, in a military policy, or in a high school administrative policy. Responses to the SIF constitute the student input data for the research program. (Copies of the SIFs and all other instruments used in the ACE studies of campus unrest may be obtained from the Laboratory for Research on Higher Education, UCLA.)

Longitudinal follow-ups are conducted by mailing questionnaires to the students' homes after they are in college. The follow-ups repeat many items from the SIF and inquire about recent experiences, particularly those having to do with college life. A typical follow-up involves about three hundred students at each institution. The campus unrest study used one-year follow-up data from the entering freshmen of 1966 and 1967. Then, in the winter of 1969, ACE, in collaboration with the Carnegie Commission on Higher Education, carried out simultaneous follow-up surveys of subsamples of the 1966, 1967, 1968, and 1969 freshmen; these were three-year, two-year, one-year, and three-month follow-ups respectively. Finally, the 1966 freshmen were again followed up in the summer of 1970 (by which time about half had completed college). The total number of students for whom both freshman and follow-up data were available was 198,285.

These longitudinal data on students were supplemented by extensive information on the intellectual, social, and administrative environments of the participating institutions, most of it already on hand in the ACE research files (see, for example, Astin, 1968; Creager and Sell, 1969). Other environmental data were collected

through ad hoc surveys completed by institutional representatives
on each campus. These were designed primarily to assess the frequency and type of unrest that had occurred during a particular
academic year and to determine whether any changes in institutional
policies or programs had resulted. Two nearly identical surveys of
this type were carried out, covering the academic years 1968–1969
and 1970–1971. A survey of the intervening academic year was
conducted using student newspapers rather than institutional representatives as the source of information.

    Case Studies. The case studies focused on detailed personal
and anecdotal information of the kind generally missing from questionnaire surveys. Thus, they had the primary goal of answering
such questions as: How do issues and demands emerge and develop
in student protests? What is the nature of the protest leadership?
How do institutional factors affect the characteristic content and
style of protest? What is the community's role in and response to
protest? How do various administrations cope with the demands of
protesters? How do protesters respond to various administrative
styles? A secondary goal of the case studies was to generate testable
hypotheses for the longitudinal studies.

    Two types of data collection were used to accomplish these
goals. One was intensive interviews with members of the academic
community. The second was detailed documentation of the most
recent protest on the campus from newspaper accounts and other
written materials.

    In selecting the sample, we used three criteria: the student
bodies of the institutions had to be diverse; each institution had to
have experienced some unrest during the 1968–1969 academic year;
and each had to be taking part in the ACE longitudinal research
program. Our definition of *protest* was "any organized activity involving members of the campus community and occurring on or
about the campus for the purpose of expressing public disapproval
of or to bring about change in some policy, practice, or event." We
were interested in various types of protests (violent versus nonviolent, institutional issue versus public issue, black leadership versus
radical left leadership, for example).

    The final sample consisted of twenty-two institutions: seven four-year liberal arts colleges (including one men's college and one women's college) ; twelve universities (five public and seven private) ; two predominantly black colleges; and one technological institution.

Thirty-five in-depth interviews were conducted on each campus with twenty-five students, five faculty members, and five administrators. The students represented certain viewpoints: five protesters, five counterprotesters, five traditional campus leaders, and ten students in general. The protesters (students who had actively participated in protests), counterprotesters (students who had actively opposed protests), and leaders (students who had held such offices as president of the student body or editor of the campus newspaper) were selected on the basis of either student or faculty nomination. The students in general were selected randomly.

On each campus, a consultant collected documents about the most recent protest and organized them according to a set of guidelines that specified form, style, and procedure. Six of the document collectors were student newspaper editors, eight were consultants outside the campus community, and the rest were faculty members or graduate students at the institution.

Studies of Campus Newspapers. A supplementary study was undertaken with funds from the Office of Education to examine reports of campus unrest in college newspapers. Newspapers from over two hundred institutions were read daily, and all incidents of unrest reported were monitored. Student newspapers have obvious advantages as a data source over the national news media and wire services, and even over local off-campus newspapers, in that their coverage is far more comprehensive, dealing with each event in the protest rather than just the more flamboyant and extreme incidents. Student newspapers are probably also a better source for such information than questionnaires completed by institutional representatives such as administrators, who cannot be expected to remember every detail of every protest that occurred during the previous nine or ten months.

The information compiled from the newspapers complemented survey findings on the incidence of various types of protests. In addition, the newspaper accounts permitted a detailed analysis of the sequence of events in protests. Although some members of our advisory committee expressed doubt about the trustworthiness of this source of information—their attitude being that student newspapers were likely to be biased in favor of protesters—the research staff felt that such a bias, if it existed, would not necessarily affect the reporting of events as they occurred. That is, a sit-in remains a sit-in whether the reporter covering the event approves of it or not; negotiations are negotiations whether a newspaper article supports the protesters or the administration. Furthermore, the validity of our data from this source was confirmed in most instances by local institutional representatives who examined the recorded sequences.

Controversy Aroused by the Study

The National Institute of Mental Health established an ad hoc advisory committee to provide expert advice and guidance to the researchers at ACE and BSSR. The advisory committee members were selected primarily for their demonstrated competence in behavioral science research and their experience with, or interest in, the study of campus unrest and related phenomena. Many disciplines (including psychology, sociology, political science, psychiatry, and education) as well as a wide spectrum of political beliefs were represented.

To gain as much lead time as possible, the advisory committee held its first meeting in the fall of 1968, before the grant application had been formally approved. The meeting was a lively one, and the topics discussed ranged from the design of the experiment to the political implications of the study. Although the meeting ended amicably, it revealed great differences among members of the committee both about how the study should be designed and about its ultimate impact. The prevailing mood at its close was one of apprehension.

The reaction of the advisory committee was our first clue that we had been naïve in assuming that the academic community would welcome a systematic scientific inquiry into the topic of campus unrest. As we began to plan the initial data collection, it gradually became obvious that—except among the ACE and BSSR research staffs, the staff at NIMH, and some members of the advisory committee—strong enthusiasm for the study was, to put it mildly, lacking. At the fall 1968 meeting of the ACE board of directors, for example, several members expressed serious doubts about the desirability of having ACE undertake such a study, their argument being that the conclusions would not be believed because the council was an arm of "the establishment." Not surprisingly, all these skeptics were presidents of institutions that had been seriously disrupted by major incidents of protest.

Since the NIMH grant was not awarded until December 1968, and since data for the case studies were to be collected the following April and May, a crash effort was needed to design and pretest the necessary instruments, to select the sample of institutions and find competent campus representatives, to train interviewers, and so forth.

Radical Student Attacks. Major responsibility for designing the interview forms was lodged at BSSR. Sometime during late March, a research assistant employed at the bureau but not directly involved in the study—a former student at a local university who had been active in Students for a Democratic Society (SDS)— "liberated" and sent draft copies of the student form, along with the names of some of the twenty-two participating institutions, to the national headquarters of SDS in Chicago.

On the basis of this information, the SDS publication *New Left Notes,* in its April 17, 1968, issue, reprinted large portions of the questionnaire along with an article ("There's a Man Going Around Doing Surveys . . .") urging its members to refuse to participate in the study because the ACE had an "insidious network of connections with the government." Such surveys, said the article, "are part of the basis for infiltration of the movement" and a means of "compiling massive dossiers about people which can be used against them for many years." It warned its readers that the BSSR was staffed by " 'liberal' pigs" who do "counterinsurgency research contract work for the U.S. government."

New Left Notes was not the only organ of the radical press to attack the study. An article in *Mayday* (March 3–10, 1969) said that ACE had "discovered a way to spot potential student 'protesters' before they are admitted to college." Armed with ACE information, admissions officers could systematically screen out protest-prone students. These two denunciations had a discernible impact on radical students (many SDS members, for example, subsequently refused to participate in the case-study interviews) and on radical faculty members, some of whom eventually persuaded their institutions to drop out altogether from the Cooperative Institutional Research Program (CIRP), the larger ACE longitudinal research program.

To add to the difficulties, in April 1969 a group of college administrators and trustees, coming together at a hastily convened meeting in Chicago to discuss the wave of unrest then sweeping the campuses, drafted "A Declaration on Campus Unrest" stating that "violence and disruption have no place on any campus." This declaration was endorsed by the ACE board of directors and released under the ACE imprimatur. Though its principal purpose was probably to discourage the repressive legislative measures then being proposed by the strategy of advocating a firmer stand against the more extreme forms of protest, its effect was to alienate students and to give apparent confirmation to the charge that ACE (and hence the office of research—although none of its staff members was involved in drafting or releasing the statement) was antistudent. One sentence in particular was widely quoted as evidence of a bias against youth: "Even in the absence of violence, there has developed among some of the young a cult of irrationality and incivility which severely strains attempts to maintain sensible communications."

Statements such as this led even the moderate National Student Association (NSA) to view ACE—and the office of research—with some distrust. In June 1969, its president, Robert S. Powell, Jr., who had in the past worked with the ACE research staff on the longitudinal program, wrote a long letter detailing NSA reservations about the unrest study. In particular, Powell expressed concern that data from the study "might be used to exclude potential protesters from institutions of higher education."

Such anxieties about the hostility of the federal government to protests were not without foundation, as evidenced by the mounting pressure in Congress for punitive legislation against protest leaders. In spring 1969, the Senate Subcommittee on Internal Security (chaired by John McClellan) had announced plans to subpoena universities for the names of student activists. This threat of a new witch-hunt appeared to validate the apprehension about the study that was expressed in the radical and student press.

Amid the growing controversy, the advisory committee met for a second time in May 1969 to discuss these attacks and to review the problems of protecting research data from government investigators and others who might misuse them for political purposes. As a result of this meeting, it issued "A Statement on Confidentiality, Use of Results, and Independence" (*Science,* July 11, 1969, pp. 158–159) affirming the need for confidentiality and backing us in our effort to ensure the security of data.

One fruitful outcome of this concern over confidentiality was the development of the link system for maintaining the anonymity of respondents (Astin and Boruch, 1970). This method protects the data from subpoena by courts and congressional committees, from unauthorized disclosure by members of the research staff, and from theft. The system was put into full operation in the fall of 1969.

The articles in *New Left Notes* and *Mayday,* which appeared just as data collection at the twenty-two case-study institutions got under way, aroused considerable resistance to the interviews, primarily at campuses with active SDS chapters. The leadership had notified members about the study and urged them not to participate. In addition, some radical faculty members became distrustful, labeled the study "fascist," and accused BSSR and ACE of conspiring with the FBI and CIA.

But even this setback had its positive side. We saw that documenting the experiences of the interviewers during this crisis might produce information helpful to future researchers of similarly sensitive topics. Moreover, the interviewers had acquired a feel for the atmosphere on campus that they were eager to communicate and that we felt would yield an added dimension to this study. We therefore sent them a semistructured questionnaire to fill out and mail back to us.

The general reception accorded the interviewers was favorable, yet almost two-thirds of them reported problems associated with the sponsorship and goals of the study. Frequently these problems were directly attributable to the articles in the radical press or to the "Declaration on Campus Unrest" endorsed by ACE. Resistance most often took the form of broken appointments; distrust, irritability, and evasiveness in responding to questions; and hostility directed at the interviewer. On one campus, interviewers encountered intense student resistance immediately after a student newspaper article quoted from the ACE-endorsed declaration. But, just the day before, two protest leaders on campus had been responsive and agreeable in interviews and had even expressed considerable interest in receiving a report of the findings.

Some 90 percent of the interviewers said that they had encountered respondents who refused to participate. Respondents who were SDS members usually gave as grounds for their refusal a belief that this kind of research would be used against their cause and that cooperation would risk exposure of their tactics. They also feared reprisals. Black students who refused to participate usually did so either because they were afraid of losing their scholarships or because they saw the study as irrelevant to their interests and goals.

In short, the generally favorable response to interviewers on most campuses was frequently marred by resistance and hostility from potential respondents. In many instances, these attitudes could be traced directly to earlier attacks on the study by the radical press or to the statement on campus unrest endorsed by the ACE board of directors. The most serious consequence was a refusal by some protest leaders (and, occasionally, by other students and by faculty members) to be interviewed. Nevertheless, we were able to interview eighty-three protest leaders on the twenty-two campuses, in part because we had completed some interviews before the study was attacked.

Radical Faculty Attacks. Data collection at the case-study institutions was completed in the spring of 1969, but the controversy continued as a new adversary entered the arena. Certain radical faculty groups (and individual faculty members) took up the cudgels against what they chose to portray as a government-inspired conspiracy to suppress dissent.

In the fall of 1969, for instance, Paul Lauter, a professor at the University of Maryland, launched a series of public attacks against the study. Lauter was on the board of directors of the New University Conference, a loose confederation of radical professors, which endorsed a resolution on September 1, 1969, stating: "There can be no question that the information gathered can be of use only to those interested in controlling campus protests—who, of course, are precisely those funding and carrying out the study. . . . The research is at best a fishing expedition, gathering massive amounts of data in the hope that some 'determinants of student protest behavior' might emerge. At worst, this government-university administration sponsored project could be construed as an intelligence operation designed to ferret out 'disruptive' elements on campus." The resolution called for ACE and NIMH to end "this wasteful and dangerous study," destroying all the data so far collected. It urged social scientists "to refuse to participate in studies like that of ACE; actively to discourage students from taking part in them; and to publicize and work to end such studies." This resolution, widely circulated in the university community, elicited a mass of correspondence from faculty members and administrators concerned about the charges and eager to learn our point of view.

The second step in Lauter's attack was a letter in the *New York Review of Books* on October 9, 1969, that called for a halt to all social science research on student behavior. Lauter asserted that such research studies "have in common the desire to understand the roots and nature of student unrest in order to control it." He exhorted his readers to "prevent this exercise in social control in the guise of social science from continuing" (p. 60). Lauter repeated many of the same charges in an article (coauthored with Archibald Alexander) in the *Antioch Review* of fall 1969 (p. 297): "The study's basic value judgment [is] that 'maladjusted' students, not inadequate, alienating, or oppressive educational institutions are central to understanding student unrest."

Attacks of this nature became a threat not just to the three-year campus unrest study but also to the ongoing ACE longitudinal program designed to explore the impact of college on students (CIRP). Six institutions that had been regular participants in CIRP refused to cooperate in the 1969 survey of entering freshmen. In at least three of these cases, "SIF burnings"—that is, destruction of questionnaires already completed by the students—were carried out.

One such incident occurred at Pomona and Pitzer, two of the Claremont colleges. It was initiated by the Sociology Field Committee, a group of faculty members from the department of sociology at Pitzer, which urged nonparticipation in the 1969 survey of entering freshmen in a general memorandum addressed to the administrations of the Claremont colleges. Their chief arguments were that the study did not provide adequate "safeguards for preserving the confidentiality of the information"; that "self-selection" by the students who participate (necessitated by the voluntary nature of the study) would tend to overrepresent the "more or less cooperative section" of the population of higher education institutions, thus biasing the results; and that the ends of the study were suspect on two grounds—that the data could be used by college admissions officers to screen out protest-prone students, and that a basic assumption of the study was that student characteristics, rather than shortcomings in the university and the larger society, were the causes of campus unrest. The memorandum concluded: "We simply cannot practice our profession in an atmosphere in which the public or critical segments of the public view us as servants of established power or any other interests in society" (p. 4).

Even though the Claremont students had already voluntarily completed the 1969 SIF, the committee was successful in persuading the faculties at Pomona and Pitzer to destroy the forms rather than return them to ACE. The Pitzer activity represented the first attack on the project initiated by fellow social scientists. Our response in this case was counterattack: we lodged a formal protest with the American Sociological Association Committee on Freedom of Scientific Inquiry on the grounds that the action of the Pitzer committee seriously infringed our freedom of inquiry. The ASA took up the matter early in 1970, but, to our knowledge, no final disposition of the case was ever made.

Yet another incident occurred at Stanford University, an institution that nonetheless remained in the CIRP. Immediately before the fall 1969 SIF was to be administered, Steve Weissman, a former radical student leader, wrote an article entitled "Testing the Freshmen: ACE Wants to Learn How to Prevent Demonstrations" for the *Stanford Chaparral* (September 25, 1969, pp. 3–4), in which he charged that, "together with ACE's National Survey of Campus Unrest, the freshman questionnaire and follow-up will provide dossiers for investigation-hungry Congressmen to subpoena 'profiles' to tell protest-wary admissions officers what kind of people to let in and what kind of people to keep out, and strategies to help college administrators manage protests and thereby postpone needed reforms. In this world, paranoia is true perception." Apparently as a consequence of this article, most of the Stanford freshmen failed to show up to take the SIF. The student press on other campuses continued to attack the study (see, for instance, "Personality Test Provokes Debate," *Cornell Daily Sun,* October 24, 1969, and "Fold, Spindle, and Mutilate," *Columbia Daily Spectator,* January 6, 1970). Though these items did not have as dire an effect as the Stanford article, they helped create a climate of distrust and fearfulness that affected students, faculty members, and administrators alike.

Right-Wing Attacks. Up to this point, attacks against the study had all been initiated by the new left. Soon after, the far right got into the act. In the *Congressional Record* of April 20, 1970, Representative John Rarick of Louisiana described the research program as "an intelligence operation—recognized by intelligence experts to be just that—which has developed information so dangerous that it is 'safeguarded' by storage in an unidentified foreign nation" (p. E3414). Rarick then read into the *Congressional Record* excerpts from a UPI-based article printed in the Baton Rouge *Morning Advocate* and an article by Frank Capell (*Herald of Freedom,* March 6, 1970), which charged ACE with close affiliation with the "subversive Institute for Pacific Relations" (and thus with having "cooperated knowingly or unknowingly in the Communist takeover of China"), with being "leftward oriented," and with having accepted "financing from questionable sources and for questionable purposes." Capell's article concluded: "Students who are throwing off more and more controls over their lives, to their detriment, should think about the possibility of control the possession of these dossiers presents. Their parents should demand the destruction of the name files and an explanation of the purpose of the questionnaires, as well as the revelation of what foreign country was selected as the repository for such confidential information" (quoted by Rarick at p. E3416).

Far from being handmaiden of the militarist-imperialist-capitalist establishment, ACE appeared from these articles to have been used by and to have used "Communists and Soviet agents." Rather than serving to screen out protest-prone students and stifle dissent, the data were being used, said the right wing, to compile "dossiers" that would serve "as guides in eliminating the 'undesirables' with reactionary tendencies and selecting those with the proper leftist views to be 'successful'" (quoted by Rarick at p. E3416).

Effects on Research. The refusal of some of the protest leaders to participate in the interviews and the loss of institutions from the CIRP were serious matters. Even more serious was the tremendous diversion of staff time and energy into activities unconnected with research. The volume of correspondence was enormous. Members of the advisory committee—several of whom had always been uncomfortable about their association with the study—engaged the staff in a series of letters and telephone calls. Reporters and free-lance writers frequently camped on our doorstep, seeking material for feature articles. (For an example of one such article, see Walsh, 1969.)

Members of the staff were also called on to discuss the project at meetings and conferences. At the time, we thought it important to take opportunities to set the record straight, despite the considerable effort required. In retrospect, this decision was probably a poor one, since most of the meetings proved fruitless, and some were even counterproductive. For instance, one "open" meeting, held at the U.S. Office of Education, was attended chiefly by hostile students who simply harassed the BSSR staff member invited to present our case. Similarly, a plenary symposium of the American Psychological Association, held in September 1969 and attended by more than 3000 psychologists, was disrupted by a dissident group who forcibly took over the platform from the ACE research director and other scheduled participants and staged their own "alternate program," which consisted chiefly of an attack on the ACE study. (For a transcript of the incident, see Korten, Cook, and Lacey, 1970, pp. 359–396.)

Every formal attack, particularly those that appeared in the "legitimate" press, seemed to demand a formal reply. Initially, we hoped to develop a standard reply, but each new attack seemed to contain unique features. Although we feared that publishing these replies would either make us look defensive or lend credibility to the attacks, we were nevertheless forced to draft replies so that we could respond to reporters or professional colleagues who inquired about their validity. These distractions from the research effort had detrimental effects on staff morale. One of the hardest ironies to accept was that a research program consciously designed to be student-centered and to help future generations of students get a better education had been attacked as a threat to students.

How much was learned from these experiences is difficult to say. Perhaps the most important lesson was that virtually no support was forthcoming from our colleagues in the social and behavioral sciences. Indeed, a number of colleagues were openly opposed to the study, and virtually no social scientists except those directly connected with the study openly defended our research. Eventually, the best response we came to hope for was indifference or neutrality. While there is no way of knowing whether a similar degree of collegial hostility and nonsupport can be expected in future studies of controversial social problems, a careful appraisal of the probable response from colleagues should probably be a routine part of the planning for such research.

II

OVERVIEW
OF THE
UNREST ERA

Student activism and campus unrest are nothing new in this country. Almost since their founding, American colleges and universities have gone through periods of turmoil and disruption. During the nineteenth century, discontent usually focused on such issues as poor food, inadequate housing, and excessively strict parietal rules; thus it was generally apolitical and parochial (Scranton Commission, 1970, pp. 21–22). In the early years of this century, radical and liberal student groups—usually affiliated with and dominated by adult political organizations and reflecting trends in the larger society—began to appear on college campuses. The Intercollegiate Socialist Society (ISS), founded in 1905, drew most of its members from higher education institutions on the eastern seaboard; it opposed rearmament and United States involvement in World War I and supported free speech on campus, immigration, and the

World Court. The Young People's Socialist League (YPSL), organized in 1907, was closely connected with the Socialist Party and worked for the election of its candidates. The Student Christian Volunteer Movement (SCVM), which included the YMCA and YWCA, at first concentrated on foreign missionary work but later took up such domestic causes as women's rights. All these groups were primarily educational rather than activist: they invited controversial speakers to campus, distributed literature, and carried out other projects well within the scope of peaceful and nondisruptive dissent. Nevertheless, World War I diverted their energies, and the Red scare that followed the war further curbed their activities (Altbach and Peterson, 1971, p. 3).

The 1920s saw renewed student activism, grounded partly in rebellion against the conventions of society and partly in criticism of the university itself. It was accused of being too big and bureaucratic and of ignoring and alienating students—charges that again became familiar during the 1960s. Many of the groups active during this period—the National Student Federation of America, the Student League for Industrial Democracy (SLID, which in 1959 changed its name to Students for a Democratic Society), and SCVM—were pacifist; they supported disarmament and protested American military incursions into Mexico and Nicaragua. The antiwar theme persisted into the 1930s, giving rise to "the first mass student movement in American history" (Altbach and Peterson, 1971, p. 6). This movement drew most of its support from metropolitan campuses, but it involved large proportions of students (more, perhaps, than the movement of the 1960s, although a much smaller proportion of young people attended college in the earlier decade, of course).

The outbreak of World War II put an abrupt end to the radical student movement. Indeed, even before the attack on Pearl Harbor, the political left, including the Communist party, was rent by internal dissensions that vitiated its strength. Following that war, efforts to organize students on a national scale were unsuccessful. Returning veterans were more concerned with taking up their studies and making good in the working world than with pursuing political goals. Moreover, the cold war and the atmosphere of the McCarthy era frustrated the attempts of the radical left—and even of liberals—to muster widespread student support. There was some faint interest on campus in such internationalist movements as the United World Federalists, some concern over civil rights (particularly after the 1954 Supreme Court decision on school desgregation), some worry about the threat of nuclear war, but the college students of the 1950s deserved the appellation "the silent generation" and the characterization "apathetic." The forties and fifties were atypical, however; radicalism and activism among students have deep historical roots. What distinguishes the past decade from earlier periods is that recent campus unrest has been student-initiated and student-centered, it has involved large numbers (if not necessarily larger proportions) of students, and it has been the subject of intensive scrutiny and widespread publicity.

Turning Points

What was it, during the early 1960s, that roused college students from their apathy? Why was the silent generation succeeded by a generation of students not merely vocal but even vociferous? While a number of underlying causes—political, economic, social, and psychological—have been proposed by many writers and theorists, our concern here is with the more immediate situational causes of extensive and dramatic campus unrest. This unrest was presaged by a number of events and undercurrents in the years immediately preceding the initial Berkeley protests. Three major issues predominated.

Early Stirrings, 1960–1964. The first—and undoubtedly the most important—issue was civil rights. In February 1960, four black students staged a sit-in at a segregated lunch counter in Greensboro, North Carolina. Their act set the pattern of nonviolent resistance that was to characterize the early stages of the civil rights movement. Soon many white students were traveling to the South to work with such organizations as the Student Nonviolent Coordinating Committee (SNCC) in freedom marches and voter registration drives. In the North, students circulated petitions, collected money, and picketed chain stores whose southern branches discriminated against blacks. Most students, whether activists or not, felt a strong sense of identity and sympathy with the cause.

The second major issue during this period was atmospheric nuclear testing. Antiwar sentiment is a recurrent theme in our history, and its manifestation in the ban-the-bomb movement of the early 1960s represents a thread of historical continuity in the student movement. These demonstrations generally ceased when atmospheric testing was ended in 1963.

The third issue that sparked student activism was the witch-hunting of the House Un-American Activities Committee (HUAC). The passive, and even craven, response of many intellectuals and academicians in the heyday of Wisconsin Senator Joseph McCarthy was changing to anger, resistance, and a reawakened concern for free speech, always a favorite campus issue. In the summer of 1960, HUAC arrived in the San Francisco Bay Area to seek out subversives, dupes, and fellow travelers. It was there confronted by loud and antagonistic crowds, among whom were students from the University of California at Berkeley and San Francisco State College. The results were the forcible removal, and subsequent arrest, of large numbers of demonstrators; the dissemination of a HUAC-sponsored film called *Operation Abolition,* which alleged that the demonstrations were Communist-inspired and that the demonstrators initiated a violent confrontation by leaping over barricades and attacking the police (the latter charge was disproved in the only case that actually came to trial); and the creation, on the Berkeley campus, of a high level of political awareness and commitment, a suitable atmosphere for the first major outbreak of campus unrest in the 1960s.

Flare-up at Berkeley, Fall 1964. The incident that touched off major unrest on the Berkeley campus was an announcement by the administration on September 16, 1964, that off-campus political groups could no longer make use of a previously "open" area—a narrow strip of university property—to hand out "advocative" literature, collect money, and solicit membership. Groups at every point on the political spectrum immediately reacted to this new stricture (actually, the revival of an old and long-unenforced rule) by forming a united front and requesting that the area be kept open. They offered to make a survey of the traffic flow (since the administration maintained that the tables manned by these off-campus groups impeded pedestrians coming to and from campus); they agreed not to solicit funds; and they volunteered to police the area to see that no group violated university regulations about posters. The administration quickly rejected the request to keep the area open. Throughout the rest of the month, students demonstrated by holding all-night vigils, staging marches, picketing the chancellor, and using other nondisruptive tactics to protest the decision. In addition, five students deliberately violated the new rules, three others supported this act of civil disobedience, and all eight were put on indefinite suspension. At this point, the Free Speech Movement (FSM) was born, with Mario Savio—one of the eight suspended students—as its spokesman.

On October 1, the most attention-getting incident in the protest took place. A nonstudent was arrested for soliciting funds for the Congress of Racial Equality (CORE), and the police car that arrived to carry him off was surrounded by hundreds of students. It remained immobilized for thirty-two hours while students gave speeches to the crowd, often climbing on the car and using it as a stage. (Eventually, students collected money to pay for damage done to the police car during this period.) October, November, and December saw continued chaos: committees were formed that issued lists of usually unheeded recommendations, the administration alternately granted concessions and imposed penalties, and students engaged in acts of protest that became more and more unruly and uncivil. A general faculty-student strike took place in December. The administration building was occupied in a sit-in, and mass arrests were made. The chancellor took a leave of absence and was later replaced. President Kerr and the acting chancellor announced, then retracted, resignations, though Kerr did indeed leave the following year. Mario Savio was suspended, jailed for 120 days by civil authorities, and later refused readmission to the university.

Although it is difficult to generalize out of this welter of events, certain significant tendencies emerge. First, as has been pointed out by a number of writers, the FSM was a kind of spin-off from the civil rights movement. Many Berkeley students had been involved in action groups in the South. Savio, who had worked in the Mississippi Summer Project of 1964, remarked: "The same rights are at stake in both places—the right to participate as citizens in a democratic society and the right to due process of law" (quoted by Wallerstein and Starr, 1971, p. xiii). Rightly or wrongly, many students viewed the administration decision of September 16 as directed primarily against civil rights groups. The tactic they used to counter this move by the university was the tactic employed in the South, namely civil disobedience. Moreover, they were convinced of the righteousness of their cause and thus of the repressiveness of the university.

The situation was difficult for the administration to handle because, in addition to campus issues, it involved off-campus issues over which the university had no control. The protesters' interference with the rights of others (for example, their occupation of the administration building and their "capture" of the police car) led the administration to call in the civil police, which bolstered the radicals' charge that the university was repressive and drew in large numbers of liberal or politically neutral students who might not otherwise have joined the protest.

The FSM actually accomplished very little institutional change. As Nathan Glazer said, four years later, "the world does look very different, and the FSM looks like a prophetic turning point; but the University of California looks very much the same"; Glazer infers from this paradox that "it is rather easier to change the world than to change the university" (1970, p. 193).

The unrest at Berkeley was exploited to the fullest by the mass media—usually with the happy consent of the protesters—and probably the extensive coverage given to the FSM, particularly to the more flamboyant and disorderly incidents, helped to account for the next stage of the student movement.

Spread of the Movement, 1964–1968. It is a gross oversimplification to attribute the spread of the student movement entirely to the press and television, however. For one thing, student activists at campuses across the nation have a way of keeping in touch with one another without the help of the mass media, and this was particularly true when Students for a Democratic Society (SDS) expanded into a powerful national organization. For another, public reaction against campus unrest, repressive legislation (or the threat of it) by the federal and some state governments, and punitive civil and institutional measures taken against protesters all served to provoke students into greater rebellion. What is most important, the drift of events in the world outside the walls of academe created concern among students and, in many cases, led to disillusionment with society as a whole and with the American political and social system in particular, thus changing the tone of student protest.

In 1964 and 1965—the years when Congress passed two bills that actualized some of the goals of the civil rights movement—the Democratic National Convention refused to seat the Mississippi Freedom Democratic delegation, Malcolm X was assassinated, and the Watts riots erupted. In 1966, when Stokely Carmichael expelled the whites who had worked with SNCC in earlier years, and Huey Newton and Bobby Seale formed the Black Panther Party, the movement turned sharply from emphasis on integration and equality of opportunity to emphasis on black separatism, black pride, and black power. During these years, too, the treatment of other minority groups—Chicanos, Puerto Ricans, and Native Americans—came to be viewed by both radicals and liberals as another harsh example of the inequities permeating American society.

The bombing of North Vietnam in 1965 sparked further anger among students. O'Brien (1971) saw protest over the war as falling into two distinct periods. The first, from February 1965 to the middle of 1967, was characterized by traditional nondisruptive tactics, including teach-ins (which originated at the University of Michigan), circulation of petitions, and mass demonstrations. During this period, support of the antiwar movement increased dramatically, and the April 1967 mobilizations in New York and San Francisco attracted three hundred thousand to four hundred thousand demonstrators. Then, beginning about mid-1967, the issues expanded to the selective service system and to university involvement—through government defense contracts and military and industrial recruiters on campus—in the war. Spontaneous protests broke out on campuses around the nation. Milder forms of dissent gave way to illegal and obstructive actions, such as interference with military-industrial recruiting and burning draft cards. The moral tone of the antiwar movement changed significantly. As the Scranton Commission (1970, p. 31) put it: "From having been a 'mistake,' the war was soon interpreted by radical students as a logical outcome of the American political system. . . . The university, too, came to be seen as part of 'the system,' and therefore it became a target—as opposed as an accidental arena—of antiwar protest."

At the same time, a new counterculture had grown up. The hippies and flower children, "youthful dropouts from middle-class environments" (O'Brien, 1971, p. 21), were themselves largely apolitical, but their existence—and the marked difference between their life-style and conventional American norms—provided a supportive base for student radicals and emphasized their antagonism to the establishment.

Between 1964 and 1968, then, campus unrest increased. At first centered in large, prestigious, highly selective institutions, it gradually diffused to colleges and universities of all types. At the same time, the scope of campus unrest enlarged to cover broad social problems rather than single-campus issues, and its direction changed. Wallerstein and Starr maintained that, after the events of 1965, the movement "began to turn against liberalism and those who embodied it—the government, the Democratic Party, and eventually college professors" (1971, p. xiii). Young people had come to distrust the political system. Many had grown discouraged about the possibility of working rationally and nonviolently to bring about necessary change, a feeling later reinforced by the assassinations of Martin Luther King, Jr., and Robert Kennedy, the riots at the 1968 Democratic Convention in Chicago, and the failure of the Eugene McCarthy forces. Finally, some had come to view the university itself as an evil instrument of the system. Thus, the stage was set for Columbia.

University as Enemy: Columbia, Spring 1968. Campus unrest at Columbia University was evident as early as spring 1965, when about two hundred students participated in an antiwar protest; such demonstrations continued in 1966 and 1967, and criticism became more sharply directed at the university itself, because of its connection with the Institute for Defense Analysis (IDA), a consortium of higher education institutions that carried out research for the Department of Defense. In February 1968, ground was broken for the construction of a new gymnasium, a project that called for the displacement of black residents of the ghetto area surrounding Columbia. At that time, the campus remained quiet, though a few neighborhood groups protested. It was not until April

23 that unrest broke out on campus. A group of black students occupied Hamilton Hall (where the administration offices of the college are located), SDS quickly joined the demonstration, and a total of five buildings were occupied and held until a week later, when city police were summoned to remove the demonstrators by force. In the ensuing melee, 707 persons were arrested, and 148 were injured. During that week, classes were suspended, and the campus remained uneasy throughout the remainder of the academic year. Late in May, white students again occupied Hamilton Hall, this time in response to the suspension of SDS leaders. The police were once more called in, and, although the buildings were cleared quickly, there was subsequent violence between students and police, with injuries on both sides. According to the Scranton Commission, the underlying issues of the protest "were Columbia's relations with the surrounding black community and [its] links with American foreign policy" (1970, p. 36).

The protest at Columbia succeeded in its immediate aims: in June the IDA severed its relations with Columbia, and in February 1969 the administration announced that plans for the new gym would be suspended indefinitely. What is more important, SDS succeeded in its aim of "radicalizing" the students—an intention allegedly announced by SDS leader Mark Rudd as early as October 1967. Daniel Bell (1968, p. 80) summarized the situation as follows: "The significance . . . was not in the number of demonstrators involved—in the first three days there were not more than two hundred fifty people in the buildings, about fifty of whom were outsiders—but in the *double* nature of the actions: tactically, the student actions had 'leaped' five years, by adopting the latest methods of these several civil rights and peace movements, which had passed, in 'five hot summers,' from protest to confrontation to resistance and to outright obstruction; even more startling, the university as a general institution, itself, was now regarded as *the enemy*, the target for disruption."

The protest at Columbia had far-reaching consequences on the course of campus unrest. During the occupation of Low Library, protesters had entered President Kirk's office and ransacked his files; later, during the second occupation of Hamilton Hall, they burned the notes of a history professor. Such actions set a pattern of property destruction and vandalism; in subsequent protests on other campuses, similar acts were committed, often at the ROTC building. Violence—on the part of protesters, counterprotesters, and police— became almost commonplace. Terroristic acts—including bomb threats, planting of bombs, and attempts to intimidate administrators and unsympathetic faculty members—also grew more frequent. Ultimately, the events at Columbia resulted in fierce public and legislative reaction against campus unrest. "By mid-1970, over thirty states had enacted a total of nearly eighty laws dealing with campus unrest," most of them punitive (Scranton Commission, 1970, p. 40).

Another significant feature at Columbia was the SDS "cooptation" (to borrow one of its favorite terms) of the protest, which had been initiated by black students. During this period and shortly thereafter, SDS was at the height of its power. By the end of spring 1969, it drew support from an estimated "fifty to seventy-five thousand students at least loosely affiliated with its hundreds of campus chapters" (O'Brien, 1971, p. 23). Then, at its June convention, members of the organization quarreled over ideology and tactics and finally split into a number of factions, the most notable being the Weathermen, a group whose extremism was repudiated by most student activists and whose deeds of terrorism and violence quickly drove it underground. Though SDS retains an organizational structure and even held a convention in 1972, it is at present moribund.

Black Militancy: Cornell, Spring 1969. Beginning about 1965, many northern colleges and universities—particularly the more prestigious—initiated active recruitment programs to enroll larger proportions of blacks, many of whom came from disadvantaged family and educational backgrounds. All too often, however, these institutions failed to plan adequately for this abrupt influx of "atypical" students, who consequently felt isolated on predominantly white campuses, neglected by the administration, and rejected by faculty members and other students. Their frequent lack of adequate preparation in high school and their relatively poor academic records and test scores—coupled with failure on the part of the institution to provide remedial courses, special programs, tutoring, and counseling—led them to feel depression, resentment, and open hostility. These feelings expressed themselves in charges of "institutional racism" and "curricular irrelevance."

As noted, whites were no longer welcomed by such organizations as SNCC. Similarly, black students on many northern campuses, impelled by a drive for separatism, presented the administration with lists of nonnegotiable demands for black studies programs, black cultural facilities, special admissions for black students, and more black faculty and staff members.

This change in mood and direction created schisms within the black community itself. For example, writing in *Newsweek* (February 10, 1969), Roy Wilkins, executive director of the NAACP, argued against this separatist tendency on the part of some blacks, contending that, "in demanding a black Jim Crow studies building within a campus and exclusively black dormitories or wings of dormitories, they are opening the door to a dungeon" (quoted by Wallerstein and Starr, 1971, p. 318). On the other side, Georgia legislator Julian Bond, pointing to the "continuing failure of the white minority of peoples in the world to share power and wealth with the nonwhite majority," maintained that black demands for separate facilities were reasonable (Wallerstein and Starr, 1971, pp. 311–319). Black students themselves were divided in their feelings; many, interested primarily in the upward mobility offered by a college education, objected to being pressured into pursuing a course that might alienate them from white society but at the same time feared being called "Toms."

Certain northern institutions that had long prided themselves on being in the vanguard of the fight against racial discrimination were suddenly faced with the allegation that they themselves were prime purveyors of a deep-rooted racism in American society. White student activists were caught in an even greater dilemma. Though in large part they owed the very existence of their organizations to the civil rights movement, though they felt a strong identification with blacks and a deep conviction about the rightness of the cause, though they had often been the victims of racist persecution in the South, they now found themselves excluded and even reviled as interfering liberal white pigs. Many continued to give support to black demands—and, in the case of SDS, to take over protests initiated by blacks—but they suffered guilt feelings and developed an almost masochistic attitude, castigating themselves for whatever part they might have played in furthering racism while refusing to drop out of the black movement.

As early as the summer of 1966, a powerful Black Student Union (BSU) was organized at San Francisco State College, and, as a result of its efforts, a black arts and culture series was established within the framework of the experimental college at that institution. But the addition of this program was considered insufficient, and demands for the establishment of a black studies program within the regular college continued. By the end of the 1967–1968 academic year, the administration had accepted the need for such a program and appointed a special coordinator, Nathan Hare, an outspoken militant whose ideas conflicted sharply with the traditional standards of the academic community. Hare proposed drastic changes in the criteria for appointing faculty members to the program and stressed that black students should be given academic credit for field work in the black community (Bunzel, 1969).

Signs of growing militancy among black students were also evident. In November 1967, a group of blacks allegedly broke into the offices of the campus newspaper and beat up the student editor. On December 6, members of the BSU occupied the administration building; police were called in, and additional violence resulted. Indeed, the troubles at San Francisco State continued through 1969, the issues expanded to cover the demands of another group (the Third World Liberation Front), and a number of secondary issues emerged—the dismissal of a faculty member who had participated in the December takeover of the administration building, police brutality, institutional sanctions against protest participants, and a ban on all demonstrations. Other campuses around the nation experienced similar explosions. In the spring of 1968, for example, Northwestern University was the scene of turmoil that had its roots in black militancy.

It was, however, the unrest at Cornell University in the spring of 1969 that brought home most strongly to the American public the element of black militancy in campus protest. Cornell was a hotbed of racial discontent. In 1963, President James Perkins had set up the Cornell Commission on Special Educational Projects, designed to recruit and provide scholarship aid to blacks. Unfortunately, Perkins made this decision without consulting faculty members and students. Consequently, the blacks enrolled under the program found themselves outside the mainstream of campus life, which was heavily dominated by fraternities and sororities. Because the university was far from large cities and the atmosphere of Ithaca was inhospitable, the black students were physically and psychologically isolated and could find a sense of community only among themselves. To add to the tension, a visiting professor of economics made a supposedly racist remark on the day of Martin Luther King's assassination; members of the Afro-American Society (AAS) demanded that he be forced to apologize, reprimanded, and dismissed; the administration investigated the matter (thus provoking the ire of the faculty, who felt their academic freedom threatened) but took no action against the professor in question (thus intensifying the frustration and resentment of the blacks).

Though plans were made in September 1968 for a black studies program, "the first to be established by a major American university" (Cohen, 1970, pp. 5–6), the newly elected president of the AAS considered that the administration was moving too slowly and presented a nine-point ultimatum demanding separate facilities. This was rejected by the university, and in response the blacks staged demonstrations that involved property disruption and the manhandling of university officials. Six activists were ordered to appear before the Cornell Student-Faculty Board on Student Conduct; the all-white composition of this judicial body exacerbated the hostility of the blacks. The citation of these students "was the turning-point in black-white relations at Cornell. For almost two months, since the militant demands for an autonomous college of Afro-American studies, interracial communications had almost exclusively taken the form of threats and insults" (Cohen, 1970, p. 8).

A crisis erupted on April 18, 1969, when a cross was burned in front of a black women's cooperative; the residents called on the administration for protection, and a single campus policeman was assigned to patrol the area. At six o'clock the next morning, black students took over Willard Straight Hall, the student union, and later that day issued a statement calling for dismissal of the charges against the cited students, separate housing facilities for blacks, and a thorough investigation of the cross-burning and of what they felt to be inadequate handling of the situation by campus police. Meanwhile, someone telephoned into the student union building to say that it was going to be bombed and that armed fraternity men were on their way to expel the blacks by force. On the strength of these threats, the occupiers had guns and other weapons brought in to them by supporters outside.

The matter was temporarily settled by negotiations between AAS leaders and the administration. Shortly after four o'clock on Sunday afternoon, the blacks left Willard Straight Hall. "The sight of students wearing bandoliers and waving rifles and shotguns dramatically demonstrated that the failure to cope with student demands might result in the loss of life and the collapse of a university community" (Cohen, 1970, p. 1).

The unrest at Cornell was by no means at an end, and the issues became even more complicated, broadening to include conflict between black students (who demanded that faculty members exhibiting racist attitudes be fired) and the faculty (who charged that their academic freedom was being violated); demands by black and white students alike for more "participatory democracy" in all aspects of institutional governance; and condemnation by all sides of administrative high-handedness in making decisions and carrying out actions without consulting other members of the academic community. But it was the widely publicized photograph of the armed blacks that stamped the deepest impress on the public mind.

Reaction and Attention. As the incidence and intensity of protest at the nation's colleges and universities grew, as disruption and violence became more typical, as demonstrators became more inflammatory and radical in their criticism of American society, public alarm and hostility increased, fanned by often sensational accounts in the mass media. No doubt the visual impact of television also helped to stir anxieties. Officials viewed protests with alarm, students and faculty members gave firsthand accounts of protest events at particular campuses, pundits of varying degrees of expertise sought to analyze the events and place them in historical context. No longer was it possible to dismiss this phenomenon as an offshoot of youthful high spirits or to blame it on a handful of wild-eyed radicals or black malcontents. Serious attention had to be paid to student protest; consideration had to be given to the possibility that charges made against the university might have some validity.

In June 1969, the board of directors of the American Council on Education created the Special Committee on Campus Tensions (known as the Linowitz Committee). Taking as its text an earlier ACE statement that "if colleges and universities will not govern themselves, they will be governed by others," the committee sought to describe the crisis, to analyze the complaints and desires of various collegiate constituents (students, faculty, administrators, trustees), and to make practical recommendations about what colleges and universities could do to restore order. At the same time, it recognized that "the higher education community cannot help to solve all the problems that create campus tensions. It cannot alone stop war, eliminate poverty, rebuild cities, or expunge racism" (Nichols, 1970, p. 36). As the Linowitz Committee was setting about its work, the administration in Washington predicted that there would be fewer disorders in the 1969–1970 academic year (*Newsweek,* September 1, 1969, p. 12). Indeed, judged solely by reports in the mass media, the fall semester was relatively calm. This "cooling down" of the campuses was more apparent than real, however, as later studies showed (for example, Bayer and Astin, 1971). Much of the protest was directed at agencies or events beyond the control of the institution rather than against institutional policies. Of particular note are the widespread observance of Earth Day (at almost two-thirds of United States institutions) and the less solid but still impressive support of the October, November, and December antiwar moratoria (discussed in detail later in this chapter). It seems obvious that students were still very much concerned not just with local campus issues but also with larger social issues—ecology and environmental pollution being relatively new themes—and, in particular, that they were still opposed to the American military presence in Southeast Asia.

Cambodia, Kent State, April–August 1970. The events of May 1970 give ample evidence of the depth of student concern and of the prematurity of predictions that "the worst of the disruption lies behind . . . or is a seasonal phenomenon" (Nichols, 1970, p. 6). On April 30, the Nixon administration announced the invasion of Cambodia. On May 4, the killings at Kent State University (Ohio) took place, followed ten days later by the killings at Jackson State College (Mississippi). The President's Commission on Campus Unrest (Scranton Commission) was established in June 1970 in direct response to these incidents. According to its report (Scranton Commission, 1970, pp. 17–18), issued in September, "During the six days after the president's announcement of the Cambodian incursion, but prior to the deaths at Kent State, some twenty new student strikes had begun each day. During the four days that followed the Kent killings, there were a hundred or more strikes each day. A student strike center located at Brandeis University reported that, by the tenth of May, 448 campuses were either still affected by some sort of strike or completely closed down."

The commission found (1970, p. 234) that "compared with other American universities of its size, Kent State had enjoyed relative tranquillity prior to May 1970, and its student body had generally been conservative or apolitical." There had been some protest activity in the fall of 1968 and the spring of 1969—and in both cases, SDS was involved—but neither protest was directly related to the events of May 1–4, nor is there any evidence that SDS or any other group of "agitators" was behind these events. President Nixon's announcement on Thursday was followed by an orderly antiwar rally on Friday and then by a weekend of restlessness, "trashing," and property destruction, climaxed by complete incineration of the ROTC building on Saturday. The mayor proclaimed a state of civil emergency, the governor backed him by issuing a number of hard-line statements, and the National Guard was called in on Sunday. The students, in the meantime, were confused by the imposition of ambiguous curfew regulations. In addition, both the authorities and the students were uncertain about the permissibility of peaceful assemblies in protest of the United States invasion of Cambodia and of the National Guard "invasion" of Kent State (as many students perceived it).

What happened shortly after noon on Monday, May 4 can be attributed in part to overreaction by public officials, in part to the lack of a clear direction and position by the university administration, and in part to growing antagonism between National Guardsmen and students. (Many guardsmen later reported that they feared for their own safety, having been the target not only of jeers and obscenities but also of stones and other missiles; many students who had previously been neutral or indifferent became resentful at having an "army" on the campus that ordered them around.) Accounts differ on the exact events that precipitated the barrage of gunfire. Despite reports immediately following the shooting, no sniper seems to have been at work, and it is doubtful that an official order to fire was given. The outcome, however, was clear enough: at least sixty-one shots were fired, leaving four students dead, nine wounded, and a nation in shock.

The events at Jackson State College ten days later were no less shocking. Indeed, it is arguable that, because the county grand jury that later investigated the incident made every effort to whitewash the city police and highway patrolmen involved in the shootings, Jackson State represents an even greater tragedy in American life than does Kent State, and one that has deeper roots than anti-Vietnam sentiment. The Scranton Commission (1970, p. 444) noted: "Jackson State is a black school situated in a white-dominated state. This is a starting point for analyzing the causes of the student disorders of May 13 and 14, 1970. The stark fact underlying all other causes of student unrest at Jackson State is the historic pattern of racism that substantially affects daily life in Mississippi." The college had been the scene of long-standing tensions: between black students and "corner boys" (black youths who were not students but who lived in the surrounding neighborhood) and between blacks and passing white motorists (the main road connecting downtown Jackson and the white residential areas runs past the college). Rock-throwing incidents were common on the part of blacks; and harassment of blacks was common on the part of city police.

The unrest at Jackson State had no direct connection with Cambodia or with Kent State, though there had been a peaceful anti-Vietnam protest on May 7. Indeed, it is not known precisely what triggered the situation on the evening of May 13, when rock throwing began, large crowds of students gathered to jeer at law enforcement officers, two trash trailers were set afire, an attempt was made to burn down the ROTC building, and rumors abounded. On the evening of May 14, three separate law enforcement groups— each with its own perception of the situation and its own training and tactics—were on the campus: the highway patrol, the city police, and the National Guard. Soon the arena of action shifted to the area outside Alexander Hall, a women's dormitory.

As at Kent State, accounts vary on the factors that precipitated the fusillade of at least one hundred fifty rounds that was fired at both the inside and the outside of the dormitory, penetrating every floor and resulting in the death of two persons and the wounding of twelve others, all black. The size of the crowd, the threat it posed, and the possible presence of a sniper on the third floor are all in dispute, but it is evident that the law enforcement officers acted without proper precaution. Moreover, their attitude was, according to newsmen on the scene, one of levity about the shooting and of contempt for blacks. Though the killings at Jackson State did not receive the same amount of attention from the media and did not have the same shock effect on the national sensibilities as those at Kent State, they were part of a pattern that turned students—many of them innocent bystanders—into the victims of the establishment, as represented by the police and the National Guard.

That pattern suffered a reversal later that summer, when a University of Wisconsin building that housed the Army Mathematics Research Center—proclaimed by radicals to be instrumental in doing research that "has killed literally thousands of innocent people" (quoted in *Newsweek*, September 7, 1970, p. 33)—was wrecked by a bomb. Not only were the computer demolished, the physics and astronomy departments seriously damaged, and the scholarly work of both professors and graduate students destroyed, but also four persons were injured and one was killed. Though bombings and bomb threats were not new to American campuses, the incident at Madison was the most extreme act of terrorism yet carried out, and, again, the one that received the most coverage from the news media. Kenneth Keniston marks the Madison disaster as a turning point, in that it brought student activists to the realization that violence and the murder of innocents were not limited to the military-industrial establishment and its academic "lackeys"; protesters themselves were capable of perpetrating outrages. Students' reactions went beyond depression and exhaustion; the mood became one of shame and embarrassment. Keniston (1971, p. 208) commented: "The emergence of violence within the movement has in turn pushed its members to reexamine their earlier self-justifying assumption that destructiveness characterized their adversaries but not themselves." It was this reexamination, according to Keniston, that accounted for the apparent calm—or, to use Kingman Brewster's phrase, "eerie tranquillity"—on campus during the 1970–1971 and 1971–1972 academic years.

Incidence

That campus unrest was on the rise from the late 1950s through the late 1960s is evidenced by Hodgkinson's fall 1968 survey (1970a, 1970b) of all presidents of higher education institutions (with a 46-percent response rate). Hodgkinson asked them to judge retrospectively whether or not they had experienced an increase in student protests during the preceding ten years. Thus, the survey extended from a period of calm on the nation's campuses (the 1957–1958 academic year) to a period of great unrest (the 1967–1968 academic year). Only 22 percent reported that no student protests had occurred at their institutions during the decade. Another 44 percent said there had been "no change," an ambiguous response that may mean, at least in some cases, no unrest. The remaining one-third reported a change in the incidence of unrest over the decade, with fewer than 2 percent of the presidents indicating a decrease rather than an increase.

Unfortunately, precise information of the prevalence of unrest at American institutions of higher education is simply not available for the years before 1968, though data from the Educational Testing Service (ETS) surveys for the 1964–1965 and 1967–1968 academic years provide a minimum estimate. These surveys did not cover two-year colleges, nor did they report the aggregate number or proportion of institutions experiencing protest. Rather, they reported in detail the incidence of protests about twenty-seven separate issues. For instance, in 1964–1965, the most prevalent issue was civil rights, with about two-fifths (38 percent) of all institutions in the survey reporting such protests. In 1967–1968, the most prevalent issue was Vietnam; again, 38 percent of the institutions surveyed reported antiwar protests. Peterson (1968a, pp. 31–32) notes that, between these two periods, not only did the absolute number of student protesters grow, but also the number of baccalaureate-granting institutions that experienced protest on each of the listed issues generally increased.

In the 1968–1969 academic year, Gaddy (1970), surveying the national population of junior colleges, found that two-fifths (38 percent) had experienced one or more incidents of organized student protest, a figure identical to the minimal ETS estimates for universities and four-year colleges in the earlier years.

The incidence of campus unrest continued to rise after 1968–1969. According to the ACE survey of 1969–1970, fully 45 percent of the four-year colleges experienced at least one incident of war-related protest. Four-fifths (80 percent) of the four-year institutions, and two-thirds (67 percent) of all institutions, including junior colleges, had protest incidents over some issue. That academic year—in which Earth Day, the Vietnam moratoria, the Cambodian crisis, and the Kent State and Jackson State killings took place—undoubtedly marks the zenith of protest activity on American campuses to date.

The next two years did not see a sharp drop in protest incidence and a return to a state of calm. The ACE survey for 1970–1971 shows that over a thousand campuses—43 percent of higher education institutions—experienced at least one protest incident. Though no comparable data are available for the entire 1971–1972 academic year, an ACE survey for the week of April 17 to 24, 1972, indicates that more than one-fourth (27 percent) of the entire academic community of some 2500 institutions had experienced protest incidents. By comparison, in the highly publicized "crisis" period of May 1–10, 1970, 16 percent of the institutions experienced protest after the Cambodian invasion, and 24 percent after the deaths at Kent State.

In spite of continuing unrest, "newsworthy" incidents have been rare since Cambodia. In part, the decline of news coverage can be attributed to the diffusion of campus unrest to institutions previously unaffected by it—smaller, less selective, and therefore less prestigious institutions—which held less interest for the national news media. The ACE surveys revealed that 40 percent of the institutions experiencing severe unrest in 1968–1969 received press coverage; in contrast, only 10 percent of those experiencing severe unrest in 1970–1971 were covered by the press. Of the 232 relatively unselective institutions (those whose students were only average or below average in academic ability) that experienced severe protest in 1970–1971, not one was mentioned in the national media. Of the 230 institutions in the high or high-intermediate selectivity range, fully forty-eight (21 percent) were the subject of reports in the news media. Although national data on the incidence of unrest since 1972 do not exist, it is clear that an era has ended.

Severity. No systematic statistical evidence on the modes, tactics, and severity of protest is available for the period before 1968. The press accounts during this period suggest that incidents of major disruption, property destruction, and personal violence were rare. In contrast, a casual reading of press accounts for the 1968–1969 academic year seems to indicate that many colleges and universities were coming apart at the seams and that higher education in general was on the brink of chaos. The ACE survey for that year, however, indicates that the mass media gave a badly distorted picture. Violence (defined by such acts as damaging or destroying buildings, furnishings, papers, records, and files and physically injuring persons) and disruption (defined by acts such as occupying buildings, holding college officials captive, interrupting classes, speeches, meetings, and other university functions, and holding general campus strikes or boycotts) were atypical modes of protest in 1968–1969. Only 6 percent of the institutions experienced any violent incidents; an additional 16 percent suffered some kind of disruptive incident.

According to the ACE survey for the "peak year" of 1969–1970, property damage and other physical violence occurred at an estimated 9 percent of American campuses. (No comparable figures are available for disruptive acts.) By 1970–1971, violence and disruption had declined—albeit only slightly—from the levels of the preceding two years: fewer than one in five of all institutions experienced either a violent or a disruptive protest. By 1971–1972, the frequency of extreme incidents was even slighter: the ACE survey of the critical week in April that followed the renewed bombing of North Vietnam indicated that no institutions had completely closed down—in contrast to the situation following Cambodia and Kent State (Scranton Commission, 1970, p. 18)—and that property had been damaged or destroyed at fewer than 2 percent of the colleges and universities.

Comparing specific modes of protest for the 1968–1969 and the 1970–1971 academic years, some acts (such as destruction of papers, occupation of buildings, and marches resulting in violence) declined at least slightly in frequency, one mode (burning of buildings) increased slightly, and other types of property destruction were as prevalent as they had been. Protests involving injury to persons were less common, as were those involving the interruption of school functions and general campus strikes or boycotts.

Institutions where severe protests took place were more likely to experience other forms of protest as well. Threats of physical violence and bomb scares, for example, occurred much more frequently at institutions that had severe protests than at other institutions. Nevertheless, at all institutions, most protest acts were mild, taking the form of presentation of demands or grievances to an established institutional body (27 percent in 1970–1971); staging of peaceful marches, picketing, or rallies (20 percent); and circulation of petitions (19 percent). Similarly, in April 1972, the most prevalent mode of protest over the renewed bombing of North Vietnam was the staging of peaceful marches or rallies (at 394 of the 685 institutions that had protests during that week); other common protest events were teach-ins and special discussion groups or seminars (126 institutions), silent vigils (99 institutions), and distributions of antiwar literature or petitions (55 institutions).

Issues. National estimates of the proportions of student protests focusing on specific issues are available for four academic years: the ETS surveys provide information on protests at baccalaureate-granting institutions (but not two-year colleges) for 1964–1965 and 1967–1968; the ACE surveys provide information on protests at all types of institutions for 1969–1970 and for 1970–1971. Although the population bases are not the same for the different years, and although the lists of issues varied slightly, the surveys are sufficiently similar to permit the identification of broad trends and changes in the issues of protest.

Clearly, the roots of the student movement do not lie primarily in antiwar sentiment; indeed, in no single year was United States involvement in Vietnam the target of protest at the majority of institutions experiencing unrest, although in 1967–1968 it was the target at a plurality (38 percent) of these institutions. According to the ETS study of 1964–1965, only one in five (21 percent) of baccalaureate-granting institutions had a protest incident about United States policies in Vietnam. Protests about civil rights, parietal rules, and food services were decidedly more common. By 1967–1968, the Vietnam issue had become dominant, but even then only 38 percent of the universities and four-year colleges had protests about this issue. Comparative data for junior college protests in the following academic year (Gaddy, 1970) indicate that, while some protest incident arose on 38 percent of junior college campuses, on only 13 percent was the Vietnam War the issue.

Even in the peak year of 1969–1970—when antiwar sentiment took the form of moratoria observances and when unrest broke out following the Cambodian invasion—protests about environmental pollution were more frequent than protests about any other single issue. Earth Day was observed at close to two-fifths (39 percent) of all institutions, more than those observing the October moratorium (32 percent), protesting war-related campus issues (11 percent), protesting general United States policy in Southeast Asia (25 percent), or protesting the Cambodian invasion (16 percent). A total of 44 percent of the campuses experienced protests resulting from the combination of Cambodia, Kent State, and Jackson State, and normal institutional activities ceased for at least a day at one-fifth (21 percent) of the institutions (Peterson and Bilorusky, 1971).

In 1970–1971, only one in five institutions had a protest about a war-related issue (United States military policy, selective service policy, or such on-campus issues as ROTC, military and industrial recruiting, and defense research). Slightly more common were protests about facilities and student life (at 22 percent of the institutions) and student power (at 27 percent). However, in April 1972, the renewed bombing of North Vietnam triggered campus unrest, primarily of a nondisruptive and legal nature, at approximately one-fourth (27 percent) of American institutions (Bayer and Astin, 1972). In short, although United States military policy (particularly in Southeast Asia) and war-related issues have been a steady source of grist to the activist mill, all other categories of issues, taken together, have evoked more protests in each academic year under consideration.

Academic and student life—a category that includes student power (a voice in decision-making), services to students, and parietal rules—has provided a focal point for student unrest in recent years. The two ETS studies show that, in 1964–1965, dormitory regulations and food services were issues of protest at one-fourth to one-third of all four-year colleges; one-fifth of these institutions experienced protests about dress regulations. In the junior colleges during 1968–1969, "situations including food service, rules on dress and appearance, student publications, and student representation in policy-making were most subject to protest activity" (Gaddy, 1970, p. 4). Moreover, accounts in the *Chronicle of Higher Education* suggest that facilities, student life, and student power have continued to be recurrent themes of protest in the academic years since 1970.

The sharpest decline over the years occurred in protests about racial issues. Civil rights (in the off-campus, local area) was the most prevalent theme of protest (at 38 percent of all baccalaureate-granting institutions) in 1964–1965; in 1967–1968, the proportion had dropped to 29 percent. On the other hand, protests about alleged racial discrimination on the part of institutions (for example, in admissions) rose from 5 percent of baccalaureate-granting institutions in 1964–1965 to 18 percent in 1967–1968. In 1969–1970, only about one in six (16 percent) of all higher education institutions had a protest about a campus issue involving race; the Jackson State killings, which occurred that same year, elicited protests at only 2 percent of the institutions. In 1970–1971, only 8 percent of the campuses experienced protest about minority group issues, usually involving special programs and special admissions policies. Of the 110 protest incidents reported in the *Chronicle of Higher Education* for 1971–1972, only 5 percent were related to racial issues.

Settings

Campus unrest was at first concentrated in a relatively small number of institutions of a particular type. An early study by Peterson (1968b) showed that such institutions tended to be large, highly selective, private, and permissive in their policies. Moreover, they attracted "protest-prone" students. What this means, as indicated in other studies (such as Astin and Bayer, 1971), is that large proportions of the students were exceptionally able academically, came from Jewish backgrounds, tended to have no current religious preference, were verbally aggressive, considered themselves political liberals, and were self-confident about their intellectual abilities. Moreover, the quality of the faculty was unusually high (as measured by the percentage who held doctoral degrees). These institutions tended to be located in the northeast or on the west coast.

Later, campus unrest became a nationwide phenomenon, spreading to various types of colleges that had not previously been affected, resulting in a "flattening out" of the relationship between institutional characteristics and protest. Nonetheless, throughout the 1960s and early 1970s, many of the same college attributes were consistently associated with the occurrence of protests on campus, particularly (in the later years) severe protests (those that involved violent incidents, such as injuries, deaths, or significant destruction of property, and those that involved nonviolent but disruptive incidents, such as the interruption of normal institutional functions and the occupation of buildings). Table 1 shows the estimated percentages of various types of institutions that experienced severe campus protest in 1968–1969 and 1970–1971, as well as the percentage that experienced protest of any kind in 1970–1971. (Data for the earlier academic year focused on violent and disruptive acts, so that no percentages are available on all types of protests.) The incidence of severe protest decreased at public universities, private universities, and four-year private nonsectarian colleges (the types of institutions that had been hardest hit in 1968–1969); it remained the same at four-year Protestant colleges; and it increased at four-year public colleges, four-year Catholic colleges, and public and private two-year colleges (the types that had previously been relatively unaffected by severe protest). Nonetheless, the rank order of institutions remained just about the same for severe protest in the years considered.

Universities, particularly private ones, were most susceptible to protests, including severe protests that often erupted in violence. Though four-year public colleges and private colleges switched their

Table 1. Incidence of Protest by Type of Institution 1968–1969 and 1970–1971

Type of Institution	Population (N)	Sample (N)		Percentage Having Severe Protest		Percentage Having Any Protest
		1968–1969	1970–1971	1968–1969	1970–1971	1970–1971
Public universities	249	54	55	43.0	35.7	73.9
Private universities	61	28	28	70.5	52.5	82.0
Four-year public colleges	343	44	45	21.7	29.4	54.8
Four-year private nonsectarian colleges	391	85	79	42.6	19.7	45.3
Four-year Protestant colleges	321	49	50	17.8	17.8	44.2
Four-year Catholic colleges	229	43	42	8.5	13.1	35.4
Two-year private colleges	230	25	22	0.0	5.2	16.1
Two-year public colleges	538	54	48	10.4	11.9	29.7
Total	2362	382	369	22.4	19.6	43.1

Sources: 1968–1969 data from Bayer and Astin, 1969, pp. 337–350; 1970–1971 data from ACE survey.

rank-order positions between 1968–1969 and 1970–1971, they too were very vulnerable to protests of all kinds. In private nonsectarian colleges, however, outbreaks of violence were rare. Protestant colleges were more likely to experience protest than were Catholic colleges, though the incidence of severe protest at the latter rose between 1968–1969 and 1970–1971, and violent incidents were proportionately more likely to occur. The two-year colleges, especially the private ones, were least susceptible to protest. These findings on the relation of educational level and type of administrative control to the occurrence of protest at an institution held fairly constant throughout the years of campus unrest.

Curricular emphasis was another characteristic found to be related to the occurrence or nonoccurrence of protest. Complex and heterogeneous institutions, such as multiversities, and (to a lesser degree) liberal arts colleges were more likely to experience protest than such specialized and single-purpose institutions as technological schools and teachers colleges. These differences are probably attributable in large part to differences in the characteristics of students and faculty members at these schools. Specialized institutions attract both students and faculty members who are more career-oriented and more conservative politically. Moreover, there is survey research evidence (see Chapter Three; Creager, 1971) that persons who major in (or teach) engineering and education are much less inclined to participate in, or even to approve of, campus demonstrations than those in the social sciences, the arts, and the humanities.

Two other institutional characteristics have been consistently related to the occurrence of unrest: size and selectivity. In general, the larger the institution, the greater the likelihood that it will experience unrest of some kind and that the unrest will involve violence and disruption. The consistent exception is the universities; those of moderate size (one thousand to five thousand students) were more protest-vulnerable than those of large size (over five thousand). This inconsistency is explained by the fact mentioned earlier that private universities, which are usually of intermediate rather than large size, were more likely to have major protests than public ones, which are larger.

Two explanations may be offered to account for the apparent causal relation between institutional size (which is closely linked to university status) and the occurrence of protest. One, labeled the "critical mass" hypothesis, was suggested by the finding (Astin and Bayer, 1971) that the *proportion* of black students at a pre-dominantly white institution was not related to the occurrence of protests over racial policies but that the *absolute number* of black students was. The implication with respect to all students is that large institutions will be more likely to have a "critical mass" of potential activists capable of organizing a protest. A second explanation (not necessarily antithetical to the first) is that the environments of larger institutions (particularly universities) have been shown to be cold and impersonal, marked by a lack of cohesiveness and by little interaction between students and faculty members, who are often more interested in their own research or in working with graduate students than in teaching undergraduates (see Astin, 1968). Thus, students feel alienated and discontented, and these feelings may manifest themselves in protest activity.

Selectivity (the average academic ability of the student body, measured by mean scores on standardized tests) is an extremely important predictor of campus unrest, particularly severe protest (Bayer and Astin, 1969). In 1968–1969, none of the least selective universities experienced severe protest, but the incidence of protest rose sharply at each successive selectivity level; by 1970–1971, 20 percent of the least selective universities experienced severe protest, and 40 percent experienced protest of some kind, but the highly selective universities still tended to suffer protest more frequently, though the increase at each selectivity level was not as pronounced. The same was generally true for the four-year colleges. The only reversal occurred among two-year institutions in the 1970–1971 academic year: the higher the selectivity level of these institutions, the smaller the likelihood of protest. This apparent inconsistency is explained by the additional fact that protest was more likely to occur at large, public junior colleges than at small, private ones, which are usually the more selective.

The close connection between selectivity (which can be considered an aspect of student input as well as an attribute of the institution itself) has also been explained in several ways. First, the students attracted by highly selective institutions are, almost by definition, more intellectual and thus probably more aware of and concerned about political and social problems; such students may use protest to express their concern. Secondly, because it brings together a large concentration of highly able students, perhaps for the first time, the highly selective institution is likely to have an extremely competitive academic atmosphere in which students are under heavy pressure to make high grades. Their resultant feelings of stress and frustration may be channeled into activist behavior. In addition, highly selective institutions attract and recruit faculty members who may influence the protest behavior of students in two ways: their frequent neglect of teaching in favor of research may create a cold and unfriendly atmosphere (like that of large institutions) that leads students to revolt; and such faculty members may also give student activism their approval or actually join in protests, further stimulating student activism (Bayer, 1971 and Lipset, 1972).

III

PARTICIPANTS

When campus unrest became a hot topic for empirical investigation in the mid-1960s, most studies focused on the characteristics of student activists, usually comparing them with nonactivists on the basis of biographical characteristics and psychological test scores. The ACE data provide a closer view not only of the student protesters but also of other significant members of the campus community. Perhaps the greatest value of these nationwide in-depth studies of students, faculty members, and administrators is their correction of some long-standing misconceptions about those who played key roles in the events that led to dramatic changes in higher education.

Students

Although various studies differed widely in their methodologies and in the kinds of students and institutions analyzed, their findings were highly consistent. Student activists emerged as more intelligent, politically liberal, individualistic, and independent than nonactivists. In addition, they were more likely to major in the social sciences, arts, or humanities and less likely to take preprofessional courses. Their interest in artistic and aesthetic pursuits was high. Their parents tended to be more highly educated, wealthier, more politically liberal, less formally religious, and more permissive in child-rearing practices than were the parents of nonactivists (Bay, 1967; Flacks, 1967; Katz, 1968; Keniston, 1968; Peterson, 1968a).

An early ACE study (Astin, 1968) tended to confirm this picture. Students who gave "none" as their current religious preference, who rated themselves high on political liberalism and low on conservatism, and who had participated in an organized demonstration while still in high school were more likely to take part in some kind of demonstration during the first year of college than the average college freshman. Other characteristics related to participation in protest were a Jewish background, a high self-rating of originality, and superior academic ability (as measured by winning recognition in the National Merit competition). Student activism was also positively related to artistic interests and goals (attending recitals or concerts, wanting to create a work of art) and to humanitarian values (wanting to join the Peace Corps or VISTA) and negatively related to such entrepreneurial goals as wanting to succeed in one's own business; this combination of attributes suggests that students who engaged in protests during college acted out of their overall convictions and values. Finally, students whose mothers were lawyers or research scientists and whose fathers were artists (or performers) or clergymen were more likely to be activists.

In the following discussion, we try to add to the picture of the student participant in protest by taking two approaches. First, we examine characteristics of the entering students that predict participation in three different types of protest. Secondly we draw on the material from the case studies to compare the characteristics of four different groups of students: protesters, counterprotesters, campus leaders, and random students.

Predictors of Participation. When campus unrest was at its height in the late 1960s, the mass media helped to create an image of the student protester as a wild-eyed, eccentrically dressed, ranting, left-wing intellectual, a knee-jerk rebel against every aspect of the system. Is there such a creature as an activist-type, ready to express dissent against all policies of an institution of higher education and against society as a whole? Or are different types of students attracted to, and moved to participate in, different types of protest? Do some issues, but not others, draw the support of a particular student? What personal and background characteristics are common to participants in all types of protests?

The data used to address these questions were obtained from two sources: student responses to the fall 1967 Student Information Form (sif), administered to entering freshmen; and responses to a follow-up questionnaire sent to the students one year later, in August 1968. The follow-up included an item asking students to indicate whether they had participated in a demonstration against racial discrimination, against some administrative policy of the college, or against the war in Vietnam. Frequent or occasional instances of participation in these three types of protests were used as dependent variables in stepwise multiple regression analyses. To conserve computing costs, the sample used for these analyses consisted of every sixth subject ($N = 5351$ students) at 178 institutions from the 1967–1968 longitudinal data.

To summarize the overall findings, the multiple Rs for all three types of demonstrations were modest: .390 for protests against racial discrimination, .342 for those against college policies, and .425 for those against the Vietnam War. This suggests that it is not possible to predict with much accuracy which students are likely to become demonstrators, and that participation may depend heavily on situational factors. Considered as a group, however, demonstrators do differ in certain consistent ways from nondemonstrators. The sif item, "What is your best guess as to the chances that you will participate in student protests or demonstrations?" proved a potent predictor of subsequent protest activity in each of the three categories. Apparently, one of the best ways of determining whether entering freshmen would take part in a protest during their first college year was simply to ask them about the likelihood. Another effective way was to look at past history. Students who had participated in some kind of protest in high school were likely to play an active role in college protests. The student participants in all three types of protests also tended either to have no formal religious upbringing or to indicate a Jewish background or preference. They also shared certain attitudes toward campus issues (opposing administrative control over student publications and disagreeing that college officials had been too lax in dealing with protests) and had in common life goals relating to aesthetic pursuits (creating such artistic works as sculptures and paintings or writing original works).

Other characteristics emerged as significant predictors in two out of three analyses. Black students were likely to participate in protests against racial discrimination and against administrative policy but not against the Vietnam War. This finding confirmed an earlier study of 1966 freshmen followed up in 1967 (Astin, 1968). Apparently, despite speculations to the contrary, black college students did not associate their concerns about racial equality with the overrepresentation of their race in armed forces combat units and their consequent concentration in Vietnam.

Participants in demonstrations against racial discrimination and in demonstrations against the Vietnam War were more likely than nonparticipants to have received National Merit recognition, to place high priority on the life goals of joining the Peace Corps or VISTA and of keeping up to date in political matters, to believe that preferential treatment in college admissions should be given to students from disadvantaged backgrounds; they were more likely to disagree that the main benefit of a college education was that it increased one's earning power.

In racial protests, students who planned to major in social science, who had well-educated mothers, and who placed little emphasis on the goal of being well-off financially were more likely to be activists. The overall pattern of characteristics suggested that a desire to work for racial equality (by demonstrating against discrimination) might have been an outgrowth either of the student's own experiences (in the case of blacks) or of a desire to help the disadvantaged (in the case of whites). Being black and being Jewish—two variables that are almost mutually exclusive—were both strong predictors of involvement in racial protests. This finding suggests not only that white students who participated in such demonstrations were disproportionately Jewish but also, by implication, that Jewish students were more socially conscious and oriented toward activism than Catholic or Protestant students.

Participants in protests against college administrative policies were differentiated from participants in the other two types of protests in that they were more likely to plan a major in fine arts, to feel that the voting age should be lowered to eighteen, to have relatively poor high school records, and, nonetheless, to have high aspirations as indicated by plans to get graduate degrees. The overall pattern of predictors suggests that this group of protesters was likely to be concerned about student power issues and to want independence from authoritarian and parental controls.

A larger number of student input characteristics entered the equation for participation in protests about the Vietnam War than entered the other two equations. This group of protesters differed from the other two groups in agreeing that organized sports should be deemphasized in college and in placing little value on the life goals of having administrative responsibility over others or making a theoretical contribution to science. In addition, antiwar protesters were likely to have grown up in a large city or in the suburbs of a large city; being male significantly predicted participation in such protests. Perhaps the most telling predictor was the antiwar protesters' inclination to say that their beliefs and attitudes were not like those of most other college students. Indeed, the general picture that emerges from this analysis conforms to the popular image of the antiestablishment pacifist who diverges from the accepted norm. Indifference to formal religion was the strongest evidence of this departure. This group also showed a pronounced inclination to reject materialistic and success-oriented goals and values and to endorse humanitarian and artistic goals.

The relation between academic ability and participation in protest is a complex one. Two variables—National Merit recognition and high school grades—tapped this dimension. The first was a positive predictor of participation in protests against racial discrimination and against the Vietnam War, and the second was a negative predictor of participation in protests against administrative policies. The most likely explanation is that academically superior students were more aware of and concerned about issues of national policy such as racism and militarism, whereas less able students were more inclined to demonstrate only about issues that affected them directly and personally.

From these analyses, we may conclude that, even though certain personal and background characteristics seem to constitute a kind of foundation for student participation in protest, participants in different kinds of protests differed from one another. Students' goals, attitudes, and other attributes as entering freshmen may predispose them to come out in support of a particular cause while they remain relatively indifferent to others.

Comparison of Protest Leaders and Other Students. The second approach taken in attempting to define the characteristics of student protesters was to examine the characteristics of protest *leaders* as revealed in interview material from the case studies. As we described earlier in Chapter One, the interviews were carried out in the spring of 1969 at the twenty-two case study institutions, all of which had experienced protests in the 1968–1969 academic year. To highlight the background and personal attributes of protest leaders (eighty-three of whom were interviewed), we compared them with three other groups of students: counterprotesters (eighty-one), traditional campus leaders (ninety-seven), and random students (one hundred eighty-five), so-called because they were selected for interviews by systematic random sampling; they might also be called students in general or typical students. Respondents in the other three groups were chosen for interviews on the basis of student or faculty nomination. Protesters and counterprotesters therefore represented the highly visible participants—those who organized, initiated, or led protests or counterprotests.

The three criterion groups—protesters, counterprotesters, and campus leaders—tended to be older than random students. At least half were over twenty-one years of age, compared to only one-fourth of the students in general. Concomitant with this finding, about two-thirds of the protesters and counterprotesters were upperclassmen or graduate students rather than lowerclassmen. Of the protesters, 22 percent came from Jewish backgrounds (compared to 15 percent of both the counterprotesters and the random students), and 45 percent gave their current religious preference as "none" (compared to 18 percent of the random students). Twenty-nine of the eighty-three protesters interviewed (35 percent) were black, compared to only 4 percent of random students. This overrepresentation of blacks to some extent distorts the findings with respect to other background factors, particularly socioeconomic status.

Earlier studies had suggested that protesters as a group came from relatively high socioeconomic backgrounds. In the twenty-two case study protests, however, the protesters were from the least affluent families. Their parents were least well educated and more likely to be employed at semiskilled jobs. Although few protesters came from families with left-wing political orientations, their parents' views were more likely to be liberal than conservative.

Protesters, like counterprotesters, tended to make high grades and to have high aspirations. About half aspired to doctorates or professional degrees, often in the social sciences. Teaching was a popular career choice. In looking to the future, however, protesters tended to be more pessimistic than other groups about their own lives fifteen years later. Although they were more likely than others to see themselves involved in social and humanitarian causes, they were less likely to foresee taking an active role in politics. Several predicted that they would probably be unhappy, dead, or in jail. These views to the future are psychologically consistent with reports on relationships of the different groups of students with their parents during the growing years. The findings of both the longitudinal surveys and the interviews on campus suggested that protesters grew up in less supportive environments and held less favorable views of their parents than did other students. Moreover, 11 percent of the protesters interviewed came from broken homes.

These findings are also consistent with the differing self-perceptions of the various protest groups, measured after the interviews by a self-administered instrument, the Adjective Check List (Gough and Heilbrun, 1965). (For a detailed report of findings, see H. Astin, 1971.) Protesters scored significantly lower than random students on personal adjustment, indicating a less positive attitude toward life and greater pessimism. They also scored lower on self-control, indicating that they were more argumentative, disorderly, and rebellious.

Protesters were much like counterprotesters in certain respects. Among men, both activist groups differed considerably from random students by scoring significantly higher on achievement (a scale relating to strength of desire to be outstanding in pursuits of socially recognized significance), dominance, autonomy, exhibition (a measure of the need to behave in ways that elicit the immediate attention of others), self-confidence, and aggression. That is, both protesters and counterprotesters saw themselves as intelligent, hard-working, forceful, and strong-willed. Both groups scored low on nurturance (a scale measuring the desire to engage in behaviors that extend material or emotional benefits to others), abasement, and counseling readiness, indicating more skepticism, self-centeredness, and self-confidence and less self-punitiveness and anxiety. This similarity between the personalities of the two activist groups supports an earlier hypothesis by Kerpelman (1969, 1972).

Counterprotesters, in large part, grew up in affluent suburban families of well-educated conservative or moderate parents. In view of their own conservative or moderate political orientation, it is not surprising to find that a large proportion cited their own parents as important influences on their attitudes about campus unrest.

Counterprotesters were more likely than others to live in fraternities or sororities and to major in natural sciences, engineering, or business. Their preferred careers were law and teaching. Fifteen years hence, counterprotesters tended to foresee personally actualized lives for themselves and to speak of their family lives, their careers, personal actualization, wealth, and success. About one in five looked forward to being politically active.

Campus leaders also came from relatively affluent homes. The fathers of four in ten were businessmen. The leaders tended to be B students with high degree aspirations; almost three-fourths were planning to get doctorates or advanced professional degrees, 30 percent specifying law. Politically, campus leaders tended to lean more to the left than the average student: 44 percent were liberal, and 22 percent left or far left.

Environmental Correlates of Participation. In Chapter Two we reviewed a number of institutional factors associated with the emergence of campus protests. Here we examine the effects of various environmental contingencies on the individual student's chances of participating in demonstrations. For this purpose we used one-year longitudinal data (fall 1967 freshmen followed up in the summer of 1968). Participation in demonstrations during the freshman year was used as the dependent variable, and entering freshmen characteristics were used as predictors. After controlling statistically for these freshman input variables, we examined a number of environmental variables in the freshman year to see if they added anything to the predictions of protest participation.

Several environmental variables appeared to contribute to the likelihood that students would protest: one was living in a college dormitory during the freshman year, and another was associating primarily with students in either the humanities or the social sciences. That dormitory living (as contrasted to living at home and commuting) should increase the student's chances of participating in campus demonstrations is not surprising, considering that dormitory residents normally spend more time on campus and become more involved in campus life than commuters (Astin, 1975; Chickering, 1974). The finding that associating primarily with humanities or social science majors increases a student's likelihood of participation is perhaps to be expected, given that majoring in these fields is a predictor of participation for students and that faculty supporters of campus protests are also concentrated in these fields (as discussed next in this chapter). Nevertheless, it should be pointed out that, since the regression analysis first controlled for the individual student's entering major, this finding probably reflects the impact of the student's environment (that is, associates) rather than simply the student's own personal predisposition.

Two other variables from the 1968 follow-up questionnaire that were strongly associated with protest participation (particularly war-related protests) were using marijuana and using LSD (or similar drugs). Since we did not have pretest measures of these items in the freshman questionnaire (and thus could not control for "input" differences in predisposition to use such drugs), it is difficult to say whether these are real "environmental" variables for protest activity. Nevertheless, these findings are consistent with the popular notion that drug use was relatively common among students engaged in radical political activity.

Faculty

Faculty members influenced campus unrest in a variety of ways. First, some faculty directly encouraged demonstrations by acting as initiators, leaders, or participants; others played an indirectly encouraging role by giving their support and approval to campus unrest. The conduct of many other faculty members (for example, ignoring their teaching responsibilities in favor of their own research, being cold and impersonal with their students) contributed to a climate that fostered discontent and frustration among students and triggered protest. Finally, the faculty and its concerns sometimes constituted the overt issue of protest. For instance, Peterson (1968b) reported that during the 1964–1965 academic year, 169 institutions experienced protests over a particular faculty member or group of faculty members. At eighteen institutions, academic freedom was the issue of protest; at another eighteen, existing tenure policies were the issue.

Attitudes toward Campus Unrest. In March 1969, an extensive survey questionnaire was mailed to a national sample of 100,315 regular faculty members teaching at 303 CIRP institutions (57 two-year colleges, 168 four-year colleges, and 78 universities, 14 of which were predominantly black). Close to 60 percent of the sample— 60,028 persons—returned usable questionnaires, and the findings discussed here are based on their responses, weighted to represent all faculty members at United States institutions of higher education. This survey was probably the most intensive (in the length of the questionnaire and the scope of topics covered) study of faculty members ever undertaken in the United States. For full marginal tabulations of all items, see Bayer, 1970.

Asked about their attitudes toward the emergence of radical student activism in recent years, faculty members were more inclined to disapprove than to approve; only 3 percent expressed unreserved approval, whereas 17 percent expressed unreserved disapproval. Approval (with or without reservations) was slightly more prevalent at four-year colleges and least common at two-year colleges. Faculty members were also asked specifically their attitude toward the most recent protest incident on their campus (in 1968–1969). About 44 percent either gave no response or said that no such incident had occurred, two-year colleges being the least troubled and universities the most troubled. When protests occurred, very few faculty members at any of the three types of institutions remained indifferent, though a substantial proportion (10 percent overall) were inclined to be uncertain about their attitudes; this confusion was most evident at universities and least so at two-year colleges. About 15 percent of the total group approved of both the aims and the methods of the protesters, another 15 percent approved of their aims but not their methods, and 16 percent disapproved of both aims and methods. Curiously, while faculty members at four-year institutions were slightly more likely to approve of the emergence of student activism generally, those at universities were slightly more likely to approve of specific protests at their own campuses.

In their responses to a series of statements that tapped general attitudes toward student activism, student freedom, and academic freedom—statements that touched on theoretical and abstract considerations rather than on concrete instances—faculty members at two-year colleges consistently proved the most conservative. Those at four-year colleges and universities expressed the most liberal viewpoints. Few faculty members at any institution agreed (either strongly or with reservations) that student political activities had no place on a college campus or that administrators had the right to control students' off-campus behavior; only about one in five felt that faculty members had the right on campus to advocate violent resistance to public authority. About 83 percent, however, agreed that faculty members should be free to present in class any idea that they considered relevant. Only 30 percent said that demonstrations had no place on a college campus. Slightly more than half the total sample felt most campus demonstrations were the work of far left groups trying to create trouble. At least four out of five agreed that students who disrupted college functions should be punished by expulsion or suspension and that campus unrest was a threat to academic freedom. Most faculty members felt that a student's grades should not be revealed to anyone off campus without the student's consent (an item that was important, at the time of the survey, because of the threat of the draft), though teachers at universities were less likely to agree with this statement than were those at either two-year or four-year colleges. Finally, 61 percent of the total group took the dismal view that respect for the academic profession had declined during the last twenty years. One may conclude that faculty members were generally in favor of freedom of expression and behavior—for themselves and for their students—as long as it did not involve disruption.

Institutional Characteristics and Faculty Influence. Data on faculty members derived from the 1969 Carnegie and ACE survey of 100,000 college and university faculty members, linked with the

ACE Institutional Characteristics File, provided an opportunity to examine the institutional correlates of faculty support of campus unrest. Four measures of faculty support were derived. The first two concerned faculty activism: the *absolute number* of faculty members at a given institution who played an active role (that is, helped to plan or organize, joined in, or openly supported) a recent demonstration; and the *proportion* of all faculty members at the institution who played an active role. The second two measures concerned faculty approval of student activism: the *absolute number* of faculty members at a given institution who said that they approved, with or without reservations, of the "emergence of radical student activism in recent years"; and the *proportion* of all faculty members at the institution who expressed complete or reserved approval.

The absolute number of faculty members who actively engaged in or approved of campus unrest was, of course, closely correlated with the size of the institution. The absolute number measures were included to test the "critical mass" hypothesis; that is, a core group of faculty may be a necessary (and sufficient) condition to influence the occurrence of a protest, whatever their proportionate numbers. A second explanation, albeit one that does not rule out the first, is the "saturation" hypothesis; that is, the proportionate number of faculty who approve of or participate in campus protest is directly related to the intensity and frequency of protest incidents. Such an index is, by definition, largely independent of institutional size.

The overall results may be summarized as follows: Faculty support of protest (in behavior and in attitude) was stronger at universities than at either four-year or two-year colleges. Faculty support was generally higher in liberal arts colleges and lower in technological institutions. Predominantly black institutions had a somewhat smaller number, but a slightly higher proportion, of faculty members who supported student activism than predominantly white institutions. Faculty members at private nonsectarian and at public institutions were more likely to support protest than were faculty members at institutions under church control, either Protestant or Catholic. Faculty support of activism was generally lower at southeastern and midwestern institutions than at either northeastern or western-southwestern institutions. The larger the institution, the greater the faculty support of activism. The higher the quality of the institution judging by any of the four measures of quality (percentage of doctorates on the faculty, library size, affluence, and selectivity), the greater the faculty support of activism.

To examine more closely the relationships between institutional characteristics and the four measures of faculty support, a series of stepwise multiple regression analyses were performed. Three institutional variables were independently related to both initiation and support of protest: size, university status, and selectivity. Again, we find the same characteristics that were earlier found related to protest occurrences.

Profile of Protester. Further analyses of the faculty survey data showed that faculty protesters had a lot in common with student protesters. Activists and supporters tended to be young (thirty-five years old or under), to come from Jewish backgrounds, to give "none" as their current religious preference, to say that they were left or liberal in their political inclinations, to be unmarried, and (commensurate with their age) to hold lower academic ranks and earn salaries of under $10,000 a year. In addition, a relatively large proportion of this group came from the social sciences or the humanities. Those who actively opposed protest and those who tried to mediate were likely to be older men at higher ranks and salaries, to be Protestant both in background and in current preference, and to be married. Furthermore, the opponents of protest were far more likely than the mediators to rate themselves as politically conservative (49 percent and 15 percent, respectively); they tended to come from the arts and humanities, the physical sciences, and "other" fields.

These findings are further confirmed by the personal interviews with faculty protest leaders ($N = 35$) and random faculty ($N = 57$) conducted on the twenty-two case study campuses. Faculty protesters were more likely to have Jewish parents (43 percent versus 14 percent), to endorse a left or far left political orientation (55 versus 18), and to be in the humanities or social sciences (77 versus 53). They also reported having more personal contacts with students and spending less time in research activities. Although faculty protesters were younger than random faculty (50 percent versus 19 percent were under age thirty-six) and had lower academic status (45 percent versus 23 percent had ranks below associate professor), a slightly higher percentage had their doctorates (74 versus 67). Faculty protesters also attended more elite undergraduate institutions (63 percent, compared to only 45 percent of random faculty, attended highly selective institutions).

Administrators

Compared to their faculty colleagues, the 101 administrators interviewed on the twenty-two case study campuses were very similar in terms of personal background characteristics. Almost 90 percent of both groups were men, about 90 percent were Caucasian, and 90 percent were married. Both groups were comparable in age (only 10 percent were under thirty years old) and current religious preference, although more administrators (80 percent) than faculty (67 percent) had Protestant parents. While administrators attended somewhat more selective undergraduate institutions than did faculty, fewer had doctoral or advanced professional degrees, and fewer were from the arts, humanities, and social sciences. Perhaps surprisingly, administrators tended to have more direct contacts with students: 31 percent of the administrators, compared to only 11 percent of the faculty, reported averaging eighteen or more hours of student contact per week. This difference may be attributable in part to the greater involvement of faculty members in research: 19 percent (as compared to only 1 percent of administrators) devoted eighteen or more hours per week to scholarly or research activities.

While administrators were frequently the principal targets of protest activity, our survey data suggest that they were often sympathetic with protesters' demands. Of the 101 administrators interviewed on case study campuses, all but 5 felt that some positive changes had resulted from student protests in the United States. When asked what these changes had been, administrators tended to report more institutional changes than either students or faculty. The most frequently mentioned changes were in the governance of the institution (42 percent) and in the curriculum (35 percent). Interestingly enough, faculty members (including those who participated in protests) were somewhat less likely to say that positive curricular changes had occurred (21 percent of random faculty and 31 percent of faculty protesters mentioned such changes).

Each of the 101 administrators reported that at least some forms of protest were acceptable to them. When asked what forms were least acceptable, administrators most frequently mentioned protests that resulted in personal injury (43 percent), property damage (43 percent), and infringement on the rights of others (43 percent). These patterns were similar to those of random faculty, but not of faculty protesters, who were more likely to mention personal injury (65 percent) and less likely to mention infringement on the rights of others (23 percent).

Questioned on how to deal with three hypothetical protest situations, administrators were more prone to look to force as a means of dealing with disruptive protests than were other members of the academic community. The hypothetical protests consisted of blocking the entrance to the administration building, preventing a guest speaker from delivering a speech by heckling, and burning down the ROTC building. Compared to all other groups interviewed (faculty and students, protesters and nonprotesters), administrators were less likely to say that they would use a conciliatory approach (finding out what protesters' demands were, inviting them in to discuss demands, asking to speak to their representatives, and so forth) and most likely to respond that they would remove the demonstrators forcefully or punish, expel, or prosecute them. In response to hecklers who prevent a speaker from delivering an address, the administrators were again least likely to say they would use persuasion and most likely to say that they would remove the protesters forcefully or punish them.

One explanation for these differences is that administrators may feel a stronger sense of responsibility to members of the academic community who may be adversely affected by disruptive protests than students or faculty feel. Considering their generally favorable attitude toward the outcomes of protests, the administrators' relatively hard line on disruptive protests suggests that they make a sharper distinction than other members of the academic community between protest *issues* and protest *tactics*. However, this greater concern with tactics has not, as we have seen, blinded administrators to the possibly beneficial results of protests.

Of course, fewer students and faculty might report positive changes resulting from campus unrest for two reasons: those who are opposed to any form of protest may see nothing but negative effects, whereas strong protest advocates may feel that the institution has been unyielding and that no changes or only trivial changes have occurred. This latter interpretation is not supported, however, by responses to the interview question concerning outcomes of the most recent protest on each campus. Fewer administrators (21 percent, contrasted to 33 percent of random faculty and 25 percent of random students) reported spontaneously that any of the protesters' demands had been met. On the other hand, administrators were somewhat more likely (14 percent) than either random faculty (12 percent) or random students (8 percent) to report that disciplinary action had been taken against the protesters. Administrators are not, apparently, inclined to take a Pollyannaish attitude about student demonstrations, simply rationalizing them in terms of positive benefits.

These results suggest still another interpretation. Could it be that administrators take a generally favorable attitude toward campus unrest as a general cultural phenomenon but are reluctant to grant that they personally have yielded to protesters' demands in an incident on their own campus? When asked to describe their role in the most recent campus protest, administrators were much more likely (34 percent) than either faculty (19 percent) or students (2 percent) to indicate that they had played a mediator role. While no faculty members and only 1 percent of the students reported being the object of an attack during the protest, 7 percent of administrators did so. On the other hand, only 5 percent reported being active supporters of the protest (as contrasted with 12 percent of the faculty and 24 percent of the students). None of the administrators and none of the randomly selected faculty reported being participants in the most recent protest, as contrasted with 12 percent of the randomly selected students. Relatively few administrators reported no involvement in the most recent protest (16 percent as contrasted with 23 percent of the random students and 30 percent of the random faculty). In short, administrators were more likely than either faculty or students to play some role in demonstrations, most often as mediators and seldom as active supporters.

Interviewers frequently commented on the great amount of *time* spent by administrators in dealing with various aspects of campus protests. (This was most often mentioned by presidents.) When asked if they felt their role had changed significantly within the last few years, most administrators (87 of the 101) reported that it had changed significantly. Of those, 29 percent felt they had less authority, 17 percent experienced more work and more demands on their time, 14 percent had to put more emphasis on public relations and mediation, and 11 percent had more student contact. Other responses were that administrators had to give more emphasis to fund-raising (5 percent), administration had become a scapegoat (3 percent), administrators needed more awareness of and interest in community involvement (3 percent), and they had a greater need for intellectual leadership (1 percent).

These responses illustrate dramatically the conflict experienced by many administrators during the peak years of campus unrest. On the one hand, there were greater demands on their time and increasing pressures for them to serve as mediators and to respond to the demands and needs of others; on the other hand, they tended to see a significant diminution of their authority to act. Thus, their capacity to deal with problems appeared to erode as the number and intensity of problems increased. As one president of a major university put it, "Trying to respond to the demands of any given constituency has become increasingly difficult, since I now find that there are increasing numbers of competing constituencies whose needs have to be taken into account."

It is also significant that only one of the administrators reported a "greater need for intellectual leadership" by administrators. That the absence of the demand for this kind of performance proved frustrating to many administrators is suggested by their answers to another open-ended question: "What do you see as the primary responsibilities of university administrators?" By far the most frequent responses concerned "providing the best educational environment for students" (39 percent) and "leadership of entire institution, coordination of all facets of the institution's functioning" (38 percent). Only 17 percent of the administrators reported "public relations" or "mediation" as primary responsibilities. This dilemma was well summed up by the spontaneous comment of a beleaguered college president: "I had always fancied myself as someone who was basically concerned with student learning and who had some pretty good ideas about how to provide effective educational leadership, but the problems of surviving from one day to the next have forced me into an entirely different role."

Summary

This overview of the various players in the drama of campus unrest suggests a number of general conclusions. First, both faculty and students who lead, participate in, or otherwise support protests show a number of traits in common: they are likely to be Jewish or to have no religious preference, to be left or liberal in their politics, and to be from the humanities or social sciences. These attributes are associated most closely with participation in antiwar protests, somewhat less with participation in racial protests, and least with participation in protests against administrative policies. Being black is associated with participation in racial and administrative protests, but not with participation in war-related protests.

Although student protesters differ markedly from counterprotesters (those who demonstrate against protests) in their political attitudes (the former being highly liberal or left and the latter conservative), both groups share a number of personality traits in common: dominance, exhibitionism, and independence. This finding supports Kerpelman's (1972) conclusion that student activism—whether of the left or of the right—can and should be distinguished from political belief.

Environmental factors can also contribute to a person's chances of involvement in campus protests. For students, involvement is more likely if the student lives in a campus residence hall and associates with students from the humanities or social sciences. For faculty, involvement is more likely in a large and relatively selective university.

Limitations in the data preclude any firm conclusions about the conditions under which administrators are likely to become involved in campus protests. Nevertheless, administrators are much more likely to get involved than either faculty or students. Their most common form of involvement is in the role of mediator. While administrators are seldom active supporters of protests, their degree of support for the protest issues and their sympathy with the protest movement in general is at least as great as that of most students and faculty members.

IV

SEQUENCES AND DETERMINANTS

How did the actions taken by the various players lead to institutional change? Although many volumes have been produced on the subject of campus unrest during the past few years, surprisingly few efforts have been made to examine the interaction of themes, events, participant groups, and administrative responses for more than a single protest. Moreover, the few protests singled out for intensive scrutiny have tended to be atypically dramatic and severe, and to have occurred at the most selective and "newsworthy" institutions. Less dramatic protests and those occurring at relatively unknown institutions have been ignored as subjects of both journalistic accounts and scholarly analytic studies. This chapter attempts to correct these shortcomings by examining antecedents and consequents of protest with the intention of identifying possible causal relationships in the protest process.

The findings result from analyses of 103 protests that occurred at sixty-seven colleges and universities during the 1969–1970 academic year. Our plan of analysis was to determine precisely the temporal *sequence* of specific events in each protest, and to estimate the probable causal connections among these events by means of a special form of regression analysis. In analyzing possible causes of any particular type of event (violence, for example), that event was used as the dependent variable (that is, it was coded as occurred versus not occurred), and only those other protest events that preceeded it in time were used as independent variables. (For a detailed discussion of the analysis procedures, see Bisconti and Astin, 1973.) All protests involved demands relating to some institutional policy: twenty-five were aimed at racial policies (such as admission of more black students), forty-one at student life policies (such as student power and parietal hours), and thirty-seven at policies relating to war (such as campus recruiting, defense research, and ROTC). To illustrate the complex maze of events that potentially lead to violence, change, or both, detailed documentations of sample protests representing each type are provided in Chapter Five.

Patterns of Protest

The three types of protests—racial, student life, and antiwar —had quite different patterns of events. Although the protests within each category were not exactly alike, certain systematic patterns were identified with respect to precipitating factors, actors, leadership, types of events, and sequences of events and administrative responses.

Racial Protests. The racial protests examined in the newspaper study were frequently continuations or recurrences of unresolved protests that had occurred during the previous academic year (see Table 2). Further, even in those cases where protest was triggered by dissatisfaction with a specific institutional policy, the issues quickly proliferated. Typically, black students presented the administration with a list of "black demands" for changes in admissions policies, more black faculty and administrators, separate facilities, and other special concessions.

The sit-in, or occupation of a building, was a common tactic; perhaps partly because of this, racial protests tended to be lengthy and to have a considerable impact on the institution as a whole, interrupting the normal, day-to-day activities of the campus: class-

Table 2. FEATURES OF PROTESTS (FROM NEWSPAPER STUDY)

Feature	Incidence (Percentage)		
	Racial Protest (N = 25)	Academic Protest (N = 41)	War Protest (N = 37)
Precipitating factors			
Dissatisfaction with university policy	92	61	89
Dissatisfaction with a specific decision or action	24	66	22
Dissatisfaction with facilities or services	40	27	—
Arrival of an industrial-military representative	—	—	54
Nonresolution of a previous protest	44	7	22
Confrontation tactics	—	—	8
Emotional or personal factors	4	7	—
Actors			
Radical left (SDS)	28	20	78
Black students	92	17	11
Police	28	17	43
Counterprotesters (YAF)	—	5	11
Students in general	84	93	70
Administrators	96	85	70
Faculty	72	56	49
Trustees, alumni, parents	8	32	3
Off-campus participants	44	24	49
Leadership			
SDS	12	7	62
Other radical left	8	12	24
Black students	92	15	—
Students in general	8	88	30
Faculty	8	10	11
Off-campus participants	24	5	11
Events			
Violence (fight, property damage, injuries)	28	15	30

	Incidence (Percentage)		
Feature	Racial Protest (N = 25)	Academic Protest (N = 41)	War Protest (N =37)
Disruption (sit-in, strike or boycott, interruption of school function, interruption of recruiting, and the like)	84	49	49
Nondisruptive expression of dissent (rallies, marches, picketing, presentation of demands)	100	88	92
Civil action	32	17	27
Institutional punitive action	36	29	43
Communications, attempts to resolve protest	100	85	65
Changes	80	59	16
Counteraction, support for administration	36	27	37
Negative response or nonresponse from administration	32	34	35

rooms were closed, concerts and lectures cancelled, the administrative routine disrupted, and so forth. Another factor that explains the general impact of racial protests on the institution was the occasional eruption of violence, an occurrence correlated with racial protests not only in the newspaper study but also in the 1968–1969 survey and the documentation study. Black students themselves, however, were involved in violence in just 6 of the 103 newspaper study protests, including 3 protests where there were fights between black and white students.

Punitive action was often one of the immediate consequences of racial protest. According to the 1968–1969 survey, it was the institution that usually took such action (for example, expulsion or suspension); the newspaper study, on the other hand, indicated that the civil authorities were the ones likely to initiate such action (for example, injunctions, arrests, or indictments), with institutional sanctions following.

Of the racial protests examined in the newspaper study, 80 percent were successful in effecting institutional change, but the changes were more likely to be partial than complete. In view of the finding (discussed below) that the sequence of disruption followed by violence predicts change, and in view of the general impact of racial protests, it seems that administrations accede to partial change largely in response to the pressure of *events*—that they attempt to resolve the problem by yielding on the more acceptable demands. The 1968–1969 survey had also suggested that disruptive and violent tactics were related to changes in racial policies. The newspaper study found, however, that changes were more likely when black students were involved as protesters, whatever the other features of the protest, which suggests that institutions were particularly sensitive to pressures from minority groups and more responsive in dealing with their grievances. Perhaps a combination of these factors is involved in the conciliatory outcome of racial protests.

Figure 1 summarizes the typical pattern of events in racial protests. The relationships were identified by means of regression analyses set up so that only antecedent events could be considered predictors (see Bisconti and Astin, 1973, for actual figures). The directly predictable outcomes—relative to other types of protest—included both violence and civil action, namely, the mobilization of off-campus police, which itself reinforced the likelihood of violence. Institutional sanctions, arrests, and a large number of events were indirectly associated with racial protests, through the mediating influence of civil action. Such protests had a widespread impact on campus life in general and were likely to result in partial institutional acquiescence to student demands.

Student Life Protests. As noted above, academic life issues constituted the most prevalent—if not always the most dramatic or newsworthy—themes of protest in the years covered by the ACE study. Indeed, though pressure for greater student participation in institutional governance is relatively recent, complaints about food services, student conduct regulations, dormitory facilities, curriculum requirements, quality of teaching, and so forth have historically been a traditional part of the college scene.

Judging from the newspaper study, protests in this category were very rarely carryovers from previously unresolved protests; most

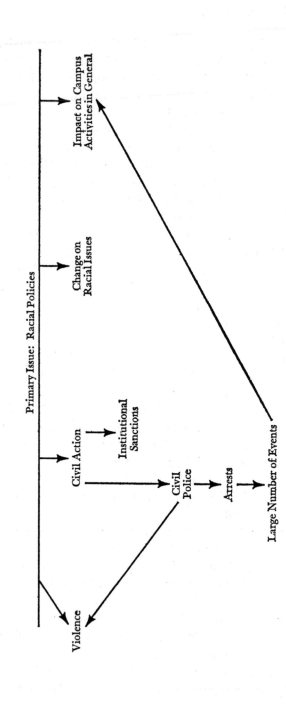

FIGURE 1. Typical pattern of events in racial protests.

were about issues that arose during the 1969–1970 academic year (see Table 2). Often, the precipitating factor was a specific administrative decision or action; other precipitating factors were general university policies and, less frequently, facilities and services.

On the whole, protests in this category were the least violent and disruptive of the three major types, possibly because the leadership was likely to be nonradical. Because of their relatively peaceful nature, few of these protests interfered with the normal processes of campus life, and police were not likely to be called in. Although administrative interest in conciliation was demonstrated by the presence of trustees in a third of the cases, and some institutional changes occurred in 59 percent, such changes were less frequent in protests about student life than in racial protests.

The two groups of protests—those about student power and those about facilities and student life—differed in some important respects. Although campus police were more likely to be mobilized in protests about student power, these tended to be less severe than protests about facilities and student life, which were more likely to be associated with violence and to result in suspension of or probation for students. A possible explanation for the milder nature of the student power protests may be provided by the finding that a conciliatory approach by the administration (studying protest demands) was associated more closely with student power protests than with those related to aspects of facilities and student life. Both types resulted in institutional changes, but changes more often occurred in response to student power issues, whereas an explicit decision against change was a frequent outcome of facilities and student life protests.

Figure 2 summarizes the common pattern of events in student power protests. The outcomes predicted by this issue were changes in student power and the use of campus police. The latter outcome predicted a large number of events that, in turn, were associated with a sharp impact on campus activities in general. Since campus police did not generally make arrests, however, these protests were less severe than those focused on facilities and student life.

Figure 3 shows the rather complex pattern associated with protests about facilities and student life. First, they were more likely to involve severe events than were student power protests, although

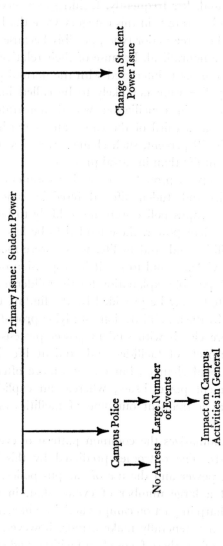

Primary Issue: Student Power

Change on Student
Power Issue

Campus Police   Large Number
of Events

No Arrests   Impact on Campus
Activities in General

FIGURE 2. Typical pattern of events in student power protests.

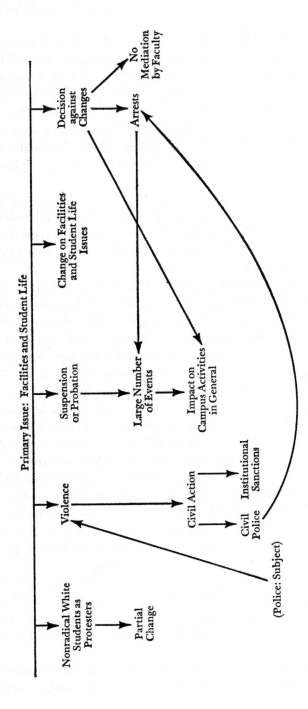

FIGURE 3. Typical pattern of events in facilities and student life protests.

the latter often lasted longer. Two separate paths—from the suspension and probation of students and from an announced decision against change—suggest the same indirectly predictable outcome: widespread impact on campus activities in general. ("Police: subject" in Figure 3 means that the presence of police was often an antecedent to the occurrence of violence.) Where violence occurred, the result was likely to be civil action followed by institutional sanctions and the calling in of civil police, which often precipitated further violence.

While change was one predictable outcome, so was an announced decision against change. Moreover, nonradical students were likely to be participants in such protests, and the typical administrative response to this group was to make partial, rather than complete, changes on a protest issue.

War-related Protests. Protests about war-related and social issues were least effective in that they received little attention and evoked virtually no administrative response. The documentation study suggested, and the newspaper study confirmed, that most of these protests were led by SDS or other radical left groups; in only 30 percent of the protests considered in the newspaper study did unaffiliated (nonradical) students play a leadership role; in no case was such a protest led by black students (see Table 2). Moreover, war-related and social protests were unlikely to garner widespread student participation; one reason for this was that these protests did not often receive the endorsement of the student government, a factor closely associated with the participation of nonradical white students. The newspaper study further suggested that the failure of students to become involved in such protests may be attributable not so much to outright antipathy against the leadership, tactics, and issues of the protests as to apathy; an aura of the commonplace surrounded the typical war-related demonstration.

General institutional policy was the dominant precipitating factor in these protests (as in racial protests). Since institutional policy regarding on-campus recruiting often came under fire, some protests were timed to the arrival of military or industrial representatives.

For the most part, the demonstrations were no surprise; in half of the thirty-seven protests examined, activities such as rallies, marches, and picketing were announced ahead of time, by either statement or advertisement. This forewarning permitted administrators to station campus police at strategic locations in one-third of the war-related protests. In some instances, plans to interrupt recruiting and to hold sit-ins or mill-ins—frequent tactics in such protests—were also publicized before the event.

In spite of the commonplaceness of and relative lack of interest in war-related protests, violence erupted in 30 percent; in 22 percent there were fights involving demonstrators, and in 14 percent property was damaged.

War-related and social protests had the smallest impact on campus activities in general and were least likely to be resolved or to lead to institutional change. Apparently, administrators preferred to ignore these demonstrations and rarely sought to negotiate or to discuss the issues. Intransigence on the part of both protesters and administrators was frequent. Moreover, faculty members were less likely to become involved, either as participants or as mediators. In short, as Figure 4 indicates, the predictable outcomes of war-related and social protests were all dead ends: no negotiations, no recommendations for compromise, and no changes, either partial or complete.

Obviously, not all protests over war-related and social issues followed this pattern. The war-research protest documented in Chapter Five was, in some ways, atypical. Though it could hardly be called an unqualified success, it was something more than the exercise in futility suggested by our general description here.

Actors in Action

We turn our attention now to the various actor groups that may be involved in a protest (though not necessarily in the role of protesters). The following sections examine the antecedent and consequent factors associated with the involvement of seven types of actors who may play roles in protest: nonradical white students, the student government, black students, sds and radical left students, faculty (in the role of protesters and in the role of mediators), the president of the institution, and the police.

Nonradical White Students. Although many people envision

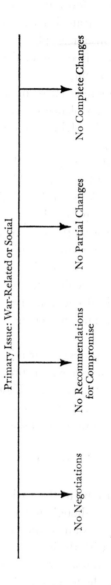

FIGURE 4. Typical pattern of events in war-related and social protests.

the typical student demonstrator as either a wild-eyed revolutionary or a militant black, the fact is that a large proportion are nonradical white students. Nonradical white students were involved in 83 percent of the protests examined in the newspaper study and actually led half.

Such students were more likely to participate when the issues concerned them directly, that is, were related to facilities and student life. They had some tendency to join protests over student power issues but to avoid protests related to racial demands.

Apparently, the "typical" student was somewhat wary of getting in too deeply. He or she was more likely to participate in protests already given "approval" by authoritative groups—those endorsed by the student government or supported by faculty members. (Indeed, one of the strongest predictors of the participation in protest of nonradical white students was the prior participation of faculty members.) Moreover, the typical student often took part in a nondisruptive expression of dissent involving large numbers of other protesters (signing petitions, or joining marches and rallies, for example), but tended to stay out of protests where the administration had threatened civil action.

When nonradical white students joined a protest, the cause was likely to be at least partially successful; indeed, partial change was the only directly predictable consequence of their participation. The relatively large protest base associated with their participation, however, had a number of important consequences. When large numbers of students participated, the administration was likely to acquiesce on a student power issue and unlikely to invoke the institutional sanctions of suspension and probation; the protest was also likely to be prolonged.

The magnitude of student support of a particular protest affected and was affected by the occurrence of three protest events: violence, police presence, and arrests. Though nonradical white students shied away from certain kinds of risks, they nonetheless tended to mobilize during or after severe incidents occurred. In particular, when arrests were made, the typical student was more likely to rally to the cause. More than a thousand demonstrators were involved in fully 64 percent of the protests where arrests occurred, contrasted with only 13 percent of the other protests. Further, in those protests involving arrests, the number of demonstrators was greater after the arrests 45 percent of the time and smaller after the arrests only 18 percent of the time. (The number was unchanged the remaining 37 percent of the time.) Similar findings occurred for police presence and violence. In view of this, and the related finding that the more students participated the more prolonged a protest was likely to be, we may conclude that calling in the police greatly increased the likelihood that a protest would escalate.

Student Government. One-fourth of the sample protests were endorsed by the student government. As we have seen, such endorsement increased the likelihood that nonradical white students would participate in the protest. In light of this relationship, it is important to understand the factors that elicit such endorsement.

The student government most frequently supported protests about academic and student life and rarely supported war-related protests. It endorsed one-fifth of the racial protests. The government was unlikely to endorse protests led or supported by the radical left or those in which the issues were couched in the form of demands. If it supported a protest at all, it usually did so early in the course of events. There was some tendency for the student government to withhold its endorsement from protests that involved police or counterprotesters. Student government endorsement was also associated with protests in which the president played some role and in which a large number of issues were raised. Finally, the student governments of large and affluent institutions were more likely to support protests.

In some ways, the student government seemed to "play it safe," the one exception being its tendency to announce a position in favor of a protest after the occurrence of violence followed by disruption. This sequence was, however, a predictor of change, so that the student government was in essence associating itself with a successful cause. Finally, in addition to promoting the support of nonradical white students, student government endorsement of protest was likely to result in change on a student power issue.

Black Students. As expected, black students were most active, both as leaders and as participants, in racial protests. Although they were rarely involved in (and never leaders of) war-related protests, they led 15 percent of student life protests. Thus, because black students were sometimes involved in protests other than those over racial policies, the pattern associated with their presence per se (Figure 5) differs somewhat from the pattern associated with protests about racial issues (see Figure 1).

Earlier ACE studies had indicated that administrators were more likely to agree to at least some changes when the protest issue was racial policy. The newspaper study further suggests that this responsiveness may have been, in part, an effort to conciliate black students. Administrators were more likely to discuss grievances with protesters (and such communications tended to forestall civil action) and to agree to at least some changes when black students were protesters. However, they were unlikely, in such cases, to agree to changes on an issue of facilities and student life, which suggests that demands for black cultural centers, separate dormitories, and the like were among those commonly rejected.

Although racial issues predicted violence (Figure 1), black student participation per se (Figure 5) was only indirectly associated with violence, the intermediary event being the use of civil police. Moreover, civil police, in contrast to campus police, were likely to make arrests. (The item "police: subject" in Figure 5 indicates that the presence of police in these protests was frequently an antecedent to violence.) On the other hand, black students often used disruptive tactics, such as sit-ins, rather than violence; indeed, disruption was related to the absence of violence. In short, since elements both conducive and deterrent to violence were indirectly associated with protests involving black students, administrative action (namely, the decision to call civil police to campus) seemed to be a key factor in determining whether violence would occur.

Radical Left Students. Members of SDS and other radical left groups were particularly active in war-related and social protests. Protests organized or dominated by radical left students tended to be repetitive and well publicized. As Figure 6 indicates, such protests were characterized by the use of campus police. The administration often posted security guards around a planned demonstration area, a move that tended to result in lengthy protests. The student government generally did not endorse protests in which radical left students played a major role, thus depriving them of one effective vehicle for mobilizing nonradical white students and for effecting change.

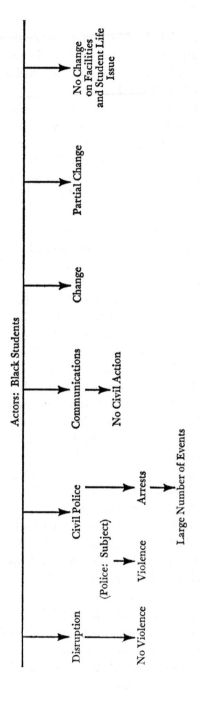

FIGURE 5.   Factors associated with black students as protesters.

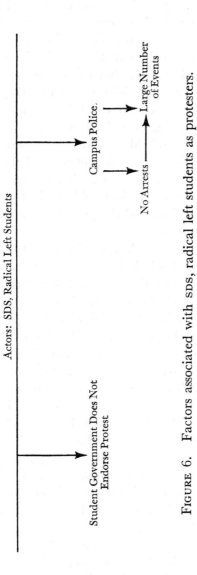

FIGURE 6. Factors associated with SDS, radical left students as protesters.

Faculty. We examined two of the roles faculty members might play in protests: participants and mediators. Faculty members were among the protesters in six out of ten protests and actually led one out of ten. Judging from the wide variety of outcomes shown in Figure 7, we may conclude that the participation of faculty members as protesters had a massive impact. The use of civil police, civil action against protesters, and violence were directly predictable from faculty involvement. Protests in which faculty members were participants tended to be lengthy and thus to have considerable impact on campus life in general. Moreover, faculty members were more likely to act as mediators in such protests, and the administration was likely to announce a decision against changes. If police were present at such protests ("Police: subject" in Figure 7), violence was more likely to follow, and the protest was more likely to have a large number of events.

As we have seen, when faculty members gave a protest "legitimacy" by engaging in it themselves, nonradical white students were more likely to join the protest. When faculty participated, student protesters rarely faced suspension or probation, although they might be subjected to other institutional sanctions and to arrest (because of the probability that the civil police would be called in).

Faculty members served as mediators in about half the protests examined. They were particularly likely to mediate in protests about racial policies. Two important consequences of their participation were discerned: civil police were unlikely to be summoned to the campus, and the administration was likely to make some changes.

Faculty tended to play a mediating role in situations where many issues were at stake, where other faculty members were active as protesters, and where the administration had neither attempted a rapprochement (by explaining its position, appointing a committee to study demands, or making changes) nor made an explicit announcement against changes. In other words, faculty mediation remained a feasible way of resolving difficulties.

If the protest involved nondisruptive expressions of dissent (rallies, picketing, marches, and the like), or if it involved the use of police with no subsequent violence, faculty members were unlikely to act as mediators, perhaps because they did not perceive the events as serious enough to require their intervention, or perhaps because

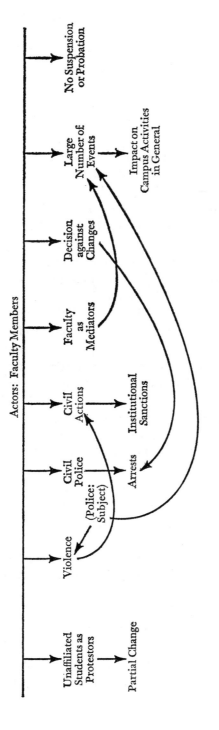

FIGURE 7. Factors associated with faculty members as protesters.

these events were often associated with war-related demonstrations, which generally elicited little response from any segment of the campus community.

President of Institution. In 57 percent of the 103 protests analyzed in the newspaper study, the president of the institution became involved at some point in negotiations or discussions with the protesters. The president was most likely to play a role in dealing with racial protests (in three-fourths of the cases) and least likely to negotiate with protesters in war-related protests (38 percent of the cases). Since the president's participation in communications was treated as a nontemporal variable in the study, it was not possible to isolate its antecedents and consequents but only to examine associated variables, without regard to sequence.

The president was likely to become personally involved in protests that were complex (had many issues) and prolonged, those in which black students participated, and those endorsed by the student government. There was some overlapping of these factors: racial protests tended to be long, and protests supported by black students and endorsed by the student government tended to have many issues. The president's involvement was most strongly associated with protests touched off by a specific administrative decision, perhaps an indication that the president was personally responsible for the decision that stirred up grievances and thus felt a greater obligation to engage directly in negotiations and discussions with the protesters.

Police. The campus security force played some role in 20 percent of the sample protests; it was particularly likely to be mobilized in war-related protests. Civil law enforcement officers were summoned to campus in 16 percent of the protests; the likelihood of their being called in was about equal for racial and for war-related protests (roughly one-fifth); in only 10 percent of the academic and student life protests did civil police play some role.

Perhaps the most important single finding from the newspaper study with implications for institutional and public policy was that police presence on campus during a protest was apparently inflammatory, often leading to violent incidents (although in most cases the police themselves were not the perpetrators of violence).

The presence of police also predicted arrests, which in turn led to prolonged protests involving large numbers of students.

The circumstances that preceded the mobilization of campus police were in some respects distinct from those that preceded the calling in of off-campus police. Whereas the latter were likely to be used when black students and faculty members were the protesters, the campus security force was likely to be present when the protesters were SDS or other radical left groups, perhaps because the radical left often publicized its demonstrations well in advance, thus giving the administration time to take precautionary measures. Campus police were also likely to be used in dealing with student power protests, which tended to be milder than protests involving black students or faculty members.

The use of either type of police force usually resulted from a situation in which communications had not been attempted and in which the administration showed itself unwilling to compromise. Campus police often became involved in protests where the administration adopted an intransigent stance and where support from the other members of the campus community (in petitions or recommendations for compromise) was lacking. Civil police tended to be involved in protests where the administration failed to explain its position, to offer to communicate, or to make changes and in protests where the faculty did not play a mediating role. It may be conjectured that violence was in some cases attributable to a sense of frustration on the part of the protesters. One further institutional characteristic was related to police involvement: the larger the institution, the more likely it was that civil law enforcement officers would be called to the campus.

Antecedents of Violence

One of the major findings to emerge from the newspaper study was the temporal relation between police presence and the occurrence of violence. Earlier studies had shown that a relationship existed but did not indicate which was the antecedent event. Thus, the question arose, "Is the mobilization of police simply a response to violence, or does the mobilization of police sometimes lead to violence?" Regression analyses based on a sequential coding determined that police presence was the antecedent of violence and not vice versa.

Factor analyses, undertaken to identify interrelationships among the protest events indicated, further, that civil police and violence were more closely related than campus police and violence. The relationship does not necessarily imply that the police themselves behaved brutally or violently. Typically, civil police were called in only when physical force (or the show of it) was deemed necessary either to restrain protesters or to remove them from a building. In such situations, physical contact between police and protesters was almost inevitable, and this—in combination with the mutual resentment that usually existed between the two groups—provided a natural setting for violence. Whatever the mechanism, however, it is clear that the administration significantly increased the probability of violence when it called on police to handle a demonstration.

Willingness by administrators to establish communications with protesters seemed to be one way of avoiding violence. For instance, when the administration established a committee to study demands, the chances that violence would occur were clearly reduced. Moreover, in no instance did violence follow after the administration made some change in response to protest demands.

Disruption was generally a negative predictor of violence. One kind of disruptive act was an exception to this generalization, however—the interruption of a school function (classes, speeches, work on construction projects, or the like). Closer examination showed that violence was rarely a direct result, but that such an interruption tended to signal a potentially severe continuing protest in which violence occurred later.

The presence of two actor groups was related to violence: faculty members as protesters visible enough to be mentioned in the campus paper, and counterprotest groups. The protest issues were another important consideration. Facilities and student life issues emerged unexpectedly as predictors of violence when other variables were controlled, although the absolute incidence of violence in such protests was low. Racial issues also predicted violence—although, when no police and no counterdemonstrators were involved, violence tended to occur no more often in racial protests than in other types of protests. Whereas scuffles with police occurred more often in war-related protests, racial protests occasionally involved fights between black and white students; in two cases, these actually precipitated the protest.

Antecedents of Change

The protests examined in the newspaper study were all directed at the institution rather than at agencies or forces outside the institution; that is, they all pressed for changes that were presumably within the power of the institution to effect. Just how successful were these protests? Looking at change as if it were a single phenomenon, we find that, of the 103 sample protests, some kind of change (complete or partial, on a primary or secondary issue) was made or explicitly promised in roughly half. The administration was most responsive to racial protests and least responsive to war-related protests. In roughly one-third of the protests, there was either no administrative response or a negative response; the proportion was about the same for all three categories of protest. In 28 percent of the protests, the administration made an explicit announcement that no change would be made.

The factors associated with institutional change tended to be closely interrelated. For instance, the combination of black students as protesters, racial issues, and a large number of issues was associated with change. Although administrators were particularly responsive to protests over racial policies, they tended to acquiesce to change whenever black students were dominant among the protesters, whatever the category of issue. The sequence of violence followed by disruption followed by change was closely associated with protests over racial policies.

Only one institutional variable—private control—was significantly related to change. The explanation may be that, in private institutions, the decision-making process tends to be less complex than in state systems, which have many levels of control (such as president, chancellor, regents, governor, citizens). Thus, the private institution can make changes more easily.

V

THREE SAMPLE
PROTESTS

Our analyses in Chapter Four indicated varying causal relationships for three types of protests: those against racial policies, those about academic and student life, and those protesting American military policy. Now we will examine a sample protest of each type to see in detail the events, participants, issues, and outcomes that illustrate some of these relationships. The three documentations of individual protests were prepared from a variety of materials, including interviews, personal observations, and newspaper reports. In the interests of greater clarity and brevity, the documentations have been rearranged and revised somewhat since they first appeared (see Astin, Bisconti, and others, 1969), and a new section on the setting has been added to each, summarizing the outstanding characteristics of the institution and its students. All data on students' socioeconomic and educational backgrounds, degree aspirations, and attitudes and values were collected in 1968.

Racial Protest: Beloit College

The following account, drawn from the case studies, documents a racial protest at Beloit College which manifested many features typical of such protests.[1] Although the protest was triggered by a specific administrative decision (the announcement that non-college persons would be banned from campus) and was followed shortly by the presentation of a list of black demands, it had its roots in previous efforts by Beloit's black students to make the college "more compatible for blacks." Indeed, in June 1968, the black students had addressed a memorandum to "concerned faculty and administration" containing a list of "requests and suggestions" that became "demands" in the 1969 protest. The protest was prolonged, extending over the first several months of the year, and had a considerable impact on campus life, involving most of the college community. The normal flow of campus life was, to some degree, interrupted by a number of short-lived sit-ins. The protest was characterized by considerable disorderliness, including property destruction and incendiarism (though the more violent acts were apparently perpetrated not by the protesters but by outsiders exploiting the situation at the college). Civil action was taken at one point—the riot squad of the municipal police was brought onto the campus—and institutional sanctions were invoked against three of the protesters. The administration and other members of the campus community were conciliatory in their attitudes, showing considerable willingness to accede to black demands and to make what adjustments they could to redress genuine grievances. Finally, the protest resulted in at least partial changes on the issues.

Setting. Beloit College, in south central Wisconsin, is a private, coeducational liberal arts college. Though originally affiliated with the Congregational and Presbyterian churches, it is, to all intents and purposes, nonsectarian. One of its most notable curricular features is its work-study program, in which students typically are enrolled for five years before receiving the baccalaureate or M.A.T. degree; they spend some semesters off campus, either studying at other cooperating institutions or doing some kind of field work.

---

[1] The documenter of the Beloit protest was James E. Jones, former coeditor of the *Round Table,* the student newspaper. Except where otherwise noted in the text, all information and all direct quotations were taken from articles in the *Round Table.* The Beloit protest documentation was not among those published in Astin, Bisconti, and others (1969), though it was included in a later (unpublished) manuscript.

Degree certification is based on examination rather than on completion of a specified number of courses. Unusually large proportions of Beloit students major in the natural sciences, journalism, political science, history, business administration, international relations, and foreign service.

Beloit is a fairly selective college (as were most of the twenty-two case study institutions), with 46 percent of its students having made B-plus or better grades in high school (compared to 29 percent of the national college population) and 19 percent having received some kind of recognition in the National Merit program (compared to 7 percent nationally). They tend to come from high socioeconomic backgrounds, as measured by parental income and education. They have high degree aspirations: in 1968, 79 percent planned to get a graduate degree (compared to 49 percent of students nationally and 74 percent of students at the case study institutions, which were an unusually selective group of colleges).

Beloit students may be described as liberal in their attitudes: an unusually high proportion agreed with the statements that students should have a major role in specifying the college curriculum and that disadvantaged students should be given preferential treatment in admissions; they disagreed that the chief benefit of a college education was that it increased one's earning power and that college officials had been too lax in dealing with protesters. Their life goals reflected similar values. They gave low priority to being well-off financially and to becoming community leaders and gave high priority to helping others who were in difficulty.

Given these characteristics and attitudes, it is not surprising to find that mild forms of protest activity had occurred earlier on the Beloit campus. Indeed, there had been a continuing effort by students to effect changes in the structure, policies, and organization of the college. For instance, they had campaigned to abolish mandatory attendance at all-college lectures and artistic performances, to reduce the physical education and language requirements, and (perhaps most important to the general student body) to win the right to determine policies governing admission to the student union. This last issue had a direct bearing on the protest documented here.

Issues. The major issue was alleged institutional racism. More specifically, black students on February 26 presented the administration with demands for:

1. Full-credit course offerings in black studies—including African and Afro-American history, art, music, philosophy, economics, government, literature, and languages—to be initiated in the summer of 1969 and taught by black professors.

2. A course on the concept of blackness, to be taken by all students, faculty members, and administrators.

3. An increase (to 10 percent) in the proportion of black students enrolled.

4. An increase (to 10 percent) in the proportion of black faculty members employed.

5. Reservation of sections of the dormitories for blacks.

6. Revision of the curriculum "to include relevant contributions by black experts in each field."

7. A black financial aid consultant.

8. A black cultural center and meeting place, to be financed by the college.

9. A high-potential education program.

10. Revision of the "area examinations" to "allow black students to relate the required courses and readings to their cultural and social environment."

11. Revision of the "common courses" to include "sections focused on blackness."

12. No further harassment of black students by clerical, custodial, and security personnel.

To a lesser degree, the issue was student power. Black students, of course, wanted to have more say in determining what was relevant to them. But many white students were also eager to have a greater role in decision-making. For example, it was felt that the students, not the administration, should decide who was to be admitted to the student union. Another issue related to student power—and one that cropped up relatively late—had to do with reform of the judicial board; though it was composed of students, its chairman claimed that it was, in essence, a "dean's board," under the thumb of the administration.

Cast of Characters. The Afro-American Union (AAU), an organization constituted under the Associated Student Senate, was dedicated to the advancement of black people and black culture both in the college and in the community. It numbered about forty blacks, not all registered students. The AAU initiated the protest by presenting demands to the administration and played an active leadership role throughout. Its main spokesmen were Mike Young (who was president), Tom Wilson, and Greg Washington (former editor of the *Round Table,* the Beloit student newspaper).

In one sense, the administration precipitated the protest by its February 1 ban of outsiders from the campus. Miller Upton, president of Beloit, was primarily responsible for that ban. Throughout the protest, Upton worked to keep the lines of communication open. The two other administrators most active in dealing with the protest were William Kolb, dean of the college, and John Gwin, dean of students. Other administrative personnel who played minor roles were Bill Carroll, chief of campus security, and Paul Pazdan, coordinator of student activities.

The student government body at Beloit, the Associated Student Senate, played a relatively minor and passive role in the protest, generally supporting the black students. Tom Schlesinger was president of the group.

The Positive Action Committee (PAC), an organization composed chiefly of white students sympathetic to the black demands, attempted to facilitate communications and cooperation between blacks and whites and to raise funds, particularly for the high-potential education program demanded by the blacks. A Faculty-Black Student Committee, originally constituted as an ad hoc group to review black demands about the curriculum and to report its recommendations to the Academic Policy Committee, was declared permanent in the course of the protest.

A six-student Judicial Board (J-Board) was called on to hear charges against three of the black protesters. Its acting chairman, Robert Arneback, declared it a "dean's board" and demanded that it be reformed.

Chronology of Events. January 20–31: The period immediately preceding the act that precipitated the protest at Beloit (namely, the president's February 1 notice) was marked by considerable disturbance on the campus by young people (nine- to sixteen-year olds, most of them black) from the surrounding community. These disturbances consisted of "vandalism, thefts, intrusion into residence halls, threats to persons, and disruption of college activities." At the end of January, the campus security log recorded an unusually large number of complaints: dorm residents objected to the excessive noise, the possibility of theft (five wallets were stolen from college residence halls), and the hostility from the young townspeople when they were questioned; professors found them stealing in the classroom buildings; and persons on campus were verbally abused and even chased. The situation was especially bad in the student union building: noise, crowding, litter; windows and recreational equipment broken; coin machines emptied; and food stolen. The administration decided, finally, "that continuation of such events was intolerable."

Saturday, February 1: Following an emergency meeting of his executive cabinet, President Miller Upton decided to ban all noncollege persons from the campus, with seven categories of exceptions (for example, persons participating in the tutoring program and persons attending public events). Dean Kolb and Dean Gwin communicated the president's decision to three leaders of the AAU, who "were either silent or nominally in assent." By 4 P.M., a mimeographed notice had been distributed to the college community; it not only announced the ban but also promised to give a full explanation of the reasons for it in the *Round Table*. (The explanation appeared in the February 3 edition.)

Sunday, February 2–Wednesday, February 5: Non-college-age youth continued to come on campus and into the union unchallenged, though they "generally acted in a quiet, orderly fashion." There was, however, some trouble. On February 5, for example, the campus security log reports that young "townie" girls harassed students in the women's restroom and did $35 worth of damage. Odell Montgomery, a black nonstudent who was active in the AAU and regarded by some as a "troublemaker," was present in the union at the time.

Thursday, February 6, 3:30 P.M.: This day was later dubbed "Black Thursday" (a phrase coined by the administration). The events began when non-college-age persons repeatedly refused to leave the union when requested to do so. At about 3:30 in the afternoon, Dean Gwin asked the black youths to meet with him in the college chapel. They complied more or less as a group; several black Beloit students were also present. White students were barred from attending the meeting, because, as Gwin stated in a personal interview, he wanted "to reduce the carnival atmosphere of the union" and to prevent the young black townspeople from having "an excuse for being black." Gwin tried to clarify the position of the administration regarding the ban, but the meeting was generally loud and disorganized. He solicited the support of the black Beloit students present; they refused to give it.

Thursday, February 6, 4 P.M.: The Beloit blacks and, a few minutes later, the town children returned to the union after the meeting. At about 4:15 P.M., Bill Carroll, chief of campus security, sent a note to President Upton (who was conducting the monthly President's Student Forum in the union ballroom) informing him that a number of non-college-age black youths were in the grill area and refused to leave. Upton immediately dissolved the forum, came downstairs, and spent the next several hours in conference with various groups—black youths, black students, deans, and faculty members—attempting to explain the reasons for the ban and to inform the young black townspeople about the possibilities for supervised youth programs on campus, especially through the sponsorship of the AAU. The city police were called around 5:15 P.M., and one car responded.

Thursday, February 6, 6 P.M.: The city police notified their riot squad to be on the alert. The grill area of the union was noisy and confused; thirty to forty town youths were there, some running about, others shouting or scrapping, others demanding food at the counter, and still others just sitting. Several policemen and one FBI agent (who had been checking on a former student for the Peace Corps) were present in the union foyer.

Around 6:20 P.M., it was announced that non-college-age youths would be arrested if they did not leave the union and the campus. Disorder prevailed. Black students became anxious, then hostile; several of them asked for a camera to photograph the police who were present. At 6:30, President Upton issued a ten-minute warning that the union was to be cleared and that anyone who refused to leave would be arrested. This announcement drew even more belligerent reactions: shouts, taunts, and threats. By this time, very few people were still seated.

About fifteen minutes later, at Upton's request, twenty fully equipped riot police entered the union and lined up in front of the service counter of the grill. Everyone, especially the young townspeople, scattered. Paul Pazdan, the administration coordinator of student activities, said later that he had been genuinely frightened. The police wore clear protective screens over their faces and were armed with clubs and aerosol spray cans of a substance like tear gas. The union was cleared and closed without violence by 7 P.M.

Saturday, February 8: President Upton issued a revised policy statement of the "use of Beloit College facilities by noncollege persons under college age," formulated after intensive consultation with the executive cabinet and with AAU representatives on Thursday night and all day Friday. Apparently, the administration had been most immediately concerned with whether the incident in the grill was a premeditated confrontation, whether it had been planned by outsiders (if it was planned at all), and who these outsiders were, if any.

The new statement, announced at a 4 P.M. forum attended by about three hundred students and fifty faculty members, administrators, and townspeople, contained four points. The February 1 ban was to be continued for two weeks until Saturday, February 22. "It is understood that this is a trial period to determine the cooperative spirit of those who have violated the order and facilities of the college. Continued violation of the policy will postpone its removal and subject individual violators to arrest and prosecution." If the policy was observed during that time period, the grill area of the union would be reopened to noncollege persons on February 22, though all other campus facilities would "continue to be off limits to anyone under college age." The reopening of the grill would be "contingent upon the willingness and ability of the student senate to organize a staff of volunteer monitors" to supervise the area. (The students consulted about this new policy statement—namely the AAU representatives and Tom Schlesinger, the president of the student senate and an ex officio member of the president's executive cabinet—had dissented on these points, feeling that they were too restrictive.) In addition, during the trial period, the AAU would "develop a program of supervised activities for community young people," while Upton would "take the lead in organizing a college-community group to move forcefully in development of a community social center for the neighborhood, to be staffed by concerned college personnel."

The discussion that followed the announcement was critical of the new policy, especially the first point. The president's argument that it would hurt both the young townspeople and the college if they were permitted to return to the union immediately (rather than after a two-week trial period) was challenged on two grounds: "The kids involved in Thursday's incident might better prove their cooperation by their presence in a supervised union than by their absence," and, since the new policy was a tacit admission that the old one had been a mistake, immediate action was needed, not postponement.

Saturday, February 8–Tuesday, February 25: During the trial period declared by Upton, non-college-age blacks continued to come onto campus. Entries in the campus security log indicated that their hostility had increased. For instance, they damaged a piano in the union ballroom, harassed security guards who were trying to lock up the building, and cut up pool tables and leather seats. There were several thefts in the union. At one point, police had to be called in to break up crap games going on in the men's room, the ballroom, and the faculty lounge.

Paul Pazdan, coordinator of student activities, said that he could not enforce the president's policy because it "had no teeth," and the youngsters knew it. (Pazdan said later that he was asked to consider resigning after he made this statement.) But the administration soon found that the policy was indeed virtually unenforceable because a warrant could not be issued unless it had the violator's name on it, and to make an arrest without a warrant required that the violator first be asked to leave and be warned of the consequences of refusal. The youngsters refused to give their names and usually ran off when police appeared.

According to the *Round Table*, "The fact that enforcement of any ban was infeasible largely overshadowed considerations that the two-week interim ban had been challenged. Therefore, the college went ahead with plans for placing the grill area of the union in an open, but 'supervised' condition." Some fifty supervisors, recruited by the student senate, were responsible for seeing that all persons in the union, whatever their age or college status, behaved in an orderly manner.

Wednesday, February 26, noon: A group of thirty-two Beloit black students walked into President Upton's office and presented him with a list of twelve demands, prefaced by the following statement: "We, the black students of Beloit College, feel these demands are imperative to our existence as useful members of the college and civil community. We feel the demands are crucial to the existence of Beloit College as a learning institution with relevance to black people."

The demands themselves (listed in our discussion of the issues at Beloit, above) called for a black studies program and other curricular changes relating to "the concept of blackness"; separate dormitory and cultural facilities for blacks; an increase in the number of black students and faculty members; and the end of harassment by various college personnel.

Finally, the mimeographed statement announced that there would be an open discussion in the union ballroom that evening. "At this time," it told the president and the administration, "we want your reply."

During the afternoon, a notice of the meeting was circulated around the campus; it said that the discussion would mean "the alpha or omega" of black-white relations at Beloit.

Wednesday, February 26, 8:30 P.M.: At the meeting that evening, Tom Wilson and several other members of the AAU told an audience of three hundred fifty to four hundred students and faculty members that, as black students of the Beloit community, they were making constructive demands on that community. Wilson read the opening paragraphs of the statement presented earlier to Upton and then called on various AAU members to explain the rationale for each demand. The speakers emphasized that they were demanding, not requesting, and cited several frustrated past efforts to work with the administration in establishing a black cultural center and recruiting more black students to Beloit.

Greg Washington of the AAU announced that he was breaking

faith with Upton by reading a letter that was intended to be read to the assembly by Gwin. The letter, which represented Upton's initial response to the black demands, asked for more time to consider each of the "proposals," in view of their far-reaching implications for "the academic program at Beloit College and its overall educational environment." Upton emphasized that the administration would move as quickly as possible. Already preliminary discussions with Kolb and Gwin and with the executive cabinet had taken place, a special faculty meeting had been called for the following Wednesday, and the matter was to be given priority at the next regular meeting of the executive committee of the board of trustees, scheduled for March 7. Upton further said that he wanted to make his response in writing "to avoid any possible misconstruing of a stated position and to permit full knowledge on the part of other students, faculty, parents, alumni, and the community at large as to what our precise position is with regard to the individual points you make and why we hold to such a position." He took exception to the use of the term *demands*: "We must all deal with one another and respond to one another in the form of proposals and requests if we wish to maintain and promote an environment conducive to progress and constructive change." The president closed the letter by inviting black students to come and talk to him about any specific points.

As he read the letter aloud, Washington inserted his own comments. For instance, of Upton's objections to the word *demands* he said: "Mr. Upton has consistently displayed an utter misunderstanding of the black person in the United States and in Beloit College. While it is unfortunate that we cannot make our demands in the form of proposals or requests, the lack of response to the needs of black students at Beloit has forced us to make demands."

When the black students had finished their presentation, John Gwin, dean of students, rose to recount the steps the administration had taken to work out programs for young people in the community. In the middle of his remarks, the black students walked out of the ballroom in a body.

After Gwin had spoken, William Kolb, dean of the college, called attention to a handout that he had prepared describing the progress of administrative efforts to carry out the "suggestions" submitted by black students in June 1968. Among other things, his statement pointed out that it was difficult to find qualified black persons for faculty and administrative positions without "raiding" the predominantly Negro institutions, that holdings in library materials by and about black people had been expanded, that some courses in black studies had been added to the curriculum, that the fall convocation cluster had been devoted to the Kerner Report—in short, that the college had not been idle in attempting to respond to black students. Kolb also attempted to clarify some of the items that one of the black students had commented on earlier and announced that there would be a special faculty meeting to discuss the black demands.

As the meeting broke up at 9:30 P.M., one white student mounted the empty stage and appealed to "concerned white students" to remain "and discuss what has just happened." This discussion later adjourned to a residence hall lounge.

Wednesday, February 26, 11 P.M.: About thirty black students assembled in front of the main dining hall, where they burned a cardboard effigy of the president and shouted the demands. Still later (sometime between 1 and 3 A.M.), forty-nine phone lines were cut at their extensions in six of the women's dormitories.

Thursday, February 27: A rally in support of the black demands was publicized throughout the day. At 10 P.M., about twenty black students gathered in front of President Upton's house and built a fire of cardboard boxes. While Mike Young shouted out each of the demands, the other black students chorused, "We demand! We demand!" Then, after two or three of the demonstrators had spit into the fire, the group marched to the student union, accompanied by about a hundred white students who had been present at the demonstration. The black students immediately retired to the Buc Room and remained there until about 11:15 P.M., forty-five minutes past the normal closing time. Sympathetic white students stayed on in the building until 11:45. The union was cleared and closed by midnight.

That same evening, the Associated Student Senate passed a resolution supporting "the spirit and specifics" of the black demands and making recommendations for implementing the changes. For instance, it suggested "that the Afro-American Union present the dean with the outline and required readings for a course on the concept of blackness"; that Dean Kolb reconsider the hiring practices of the college, particularly the possibility of "recruiting *qualified* but formally unaccredited black faculty"; and that all students discuss the demands formally with faculty and administration and informally among themselves and vote on the black demands in a forthcoming senate opinion poll.

Friday, February 28: In the middle of an evening lecture on the Cuban Revolution by Professor Ruiz of Smith College, four black students walked in, took over the microphone, read out the demands, and walked out again, to the beat of jungle drums.

Later, a group of seven or eight black students met by appointment with President Upton. They read him a list of plans for implementing the demands, which was later printed in the *Round Table* along with a prefatory note stating: "These plans should be viewed in the same light as our demands. They are not suggestions or proposals. They are the way we want it done. Any discussion will have to start from our implementation plans." Principally, the students asked for increased representation on the committees considering the various demands. They said, for instance, that to implement the first demand (black studies), black representatives should be included on the Academic Policy Committee, should talk to department chairmen and attend departmental meetings to discuss specific courses, and should attend all faculty meetings on a nonvoting basis.

Saturday, March 1, 3 P.M.: The participants in the Cuban Convocation Cluster, in its afternoon session, put aside their announced topic and instead talked about the black demands. According to a news analyst in the *Round Table,* the main point that emerged from this discussion was "that the institutional racism in Beloit College is not unique to the college but to the entire white American culture." One participant, Professor Zeitlin, remarked that "prejudice is an institution in America, not merely a social problem [as it is in Cuba]." Saul Landau, another participant, said that the demands were not revolutionary but reasonable and just and "indeed, perhaps so simple that they're too frightening to be heard." The panelists all felt that the major issue was whether the white community had the determination to implement the demands.

Sunday, March 2: A group of black students remained in

the library past the normal closing hour of 11 P.M., on the ground that they needed to catch up on their studies. In a later memorandum addressed to parents, President Upton reported, "Dean Gwin, in consultation with me, agreed to this and sat with them until 7:15 A.M. when they left of their own volition. Most of the time was spent in study and napping. There was no disturbance or disruption."

The same evening, the student government's dorm council passed a recommendation that separate facilities be set aside in dormitories for those black students who wanted them, that students not be eligible for this separate living area until their third term, and that "residence in these separate areas be on a voluntary basis only."

Tuesday, March 4, evening: About twenty persons, mostly high-school-age blacks, refused to leave the union. They staged a sit-in as a gesture of support of the black demands until 11:30, when they left peaceably.

Wednesday, March 5, 1:20 A.M.: Three firebombs were thrown through a rear window into the college infirmary, causing about $1500 worth of damage. No one was hurt, since the infirmary was not occupied at night. At about the same time, someone called in a false alarm about a fire in the library.

Wednesday, March 5, 4 P.M.: Immediately before a special faculty meeting that had been called to discuss the black demands, a small group of black students, wearing African dress and carrying conga drums, gathered in the lobby of Morse-Ingersoll Hall, where the meeting was to take place. The faculty discussed the demands for two hours that afternoon and met again that evening for several hours.

Thursday, March 6, evening: At 10 P.M., about twenty black students demonstrated in front of the president's house and then went to the union, where they sat in—along with some thirty-five white students and nonstudents—until midnight.

Sometime between 9 and 11 P.M., the sinks in the men's room on the top floor of the library were stopped up, and the water was turned on. Campus security personnel discovered the overflow at 11 P.M. The periodicals section on the main floor received slight damage.

Friday, March 7, 4:15 A.M.: A fire was reported in Porter Residence Hall, one of a complex of new dormitories housing sixty women. According to a release from the president's office, "fires were set in about ten of the small dating parlors by putting a plastic spoon in a paper cup filled with gum turpentine and placed under a stuffed sofa or chair. The spoon acted as a wick. Two of the parlors were completely destroyed, the heat triggered the fire alarm, and prayerfully no personal injury was suffered." There was considerable smoke damage in the hall, especially in the stairwells.

Later that day, the office of the president released a statement addressed to "all members of the Beloit College community." One paragraph read: "It is all-important that these incendiary incidents not be identified with the campus controversy surrounding the Black student demands and my response. The campus tensions produced by this controversy are simply being exploited by a sick mentality for the sake of gratifying a latent tendency to engage in criminal arson. There is probably no more serious crime than that of igniting the lower floors of a residence hall during sleeping hours. Regardless of differences that might prevail among members of the community with regard to campus issues, we must all be joined in the prevention of any repetition of such an act and in the prompt identification of those who would commit such an act." Upton also urged the college community to refrain from gossip and "speculative conversation of any sort," since that would only increase general tension and anxiety and thus play into "the sick designs of a depraved mentality."

Friday, March 7, 9 P.M.: President Upton presented to AAU representatives a document detailing his response to the black demands; the document was released a few hours later to the general college community. It opened by expressing the hope that the word *demands* reflected the black students' "conception of the urgency and justness of your proposals" and was not used in the sense of "preemptory items about which there can be no disagreement or discussion, only acceptance." Next it expressed respect and admiration for the blacks: "You have much to offer the rest of us, and we so earnestly want to reach out and be part of your life. . . . We therefore hope fervently that you will not deny us this opportunity by placing us in the untenable position of having either to abdicate our own values or exclude you from our midst."

Upton then responded point by point to the black demands, generally in favorable but heavily qualified terms. Only one demand—that sections of the dormitories be reserved for black students—was flatly turned down, on the ground that "segregated student housing is in violation of the Civil Rights Act of 1964." But, the president added, it would be possible for a group of students to apply to the dean of students "for group housing on a nonsegregated basis."

Three demands were to be implemented immediately: a black counselor who could also advise students in financial matters was to be hired, a black cultural center and meeting place was to be set up (with the proviso that it not be segregated), and a judicial body was to be established to investigate charges of harassment by college employees.

With respect to other demands, the president's response was more equivocal. In some cases, he objected to underlying assumptions. Of the first demand (for a full black studies program, with all courses to be taught by black professors), he said: "There is good reason to seriously question your statement that 'the very nature of these courses requires that they be taught by black professors.' Black teachers might be able to bring a valuable 'internal' perspective on Afro-American history and a new 'internal' perspective on American history. But white teachers might bring an external and empathic perspective that is equally valuable. Neither specialized competence can be viewed as decisive." Upton also pointed out that a number of black studies courses already existed but added that the need for more courses would be reexamined. He gave similar replies to the demands for curriculum reevaluation and for revision of the common courses.

In reply to the demands for larger proportions of black students and faculty members, the president noted practical difficulties. Lack of finances and staff, he said, prevented the immediate establishment of the high-potential education program.

Black students were urged to be more specific about some demands and to take more initiative in coping with the practical problems. Acknowledging that a course in the concept of blackness seemed a reasonable request and that many people in the college community would be interested in such a course, he urged that the black students "prepare a detailed course proposal that would suggest your position regarding a mandatory course, and then bring it to the attention of the faculty for consideration and action"; in the interim, he suggested that they organize seminars to be attended voluntarily.

The statement closed by challenging the black students to help develop "a videotape or other audiovisual program in various black subjects, which could utilize the best black scholars in the country involved with students at Beloit." The administration would seek funds for such a project and would otherwise work toward it, but it needed the impetus of the black students themselves, the president said.

At 3 P.M., about twenty black students demonstrated in front of Chapin Hall, where the college trustees were holding their winter meeting. The blacks beat drums and burned an effigy of the president.

Sunday, March 9: After several meetings throughout the week, the faculty released a statement expressing sympathy with the black demands and at the same time endorsing most of President Upton's specific responses. Its major contribution was the proposal that a special ad hoc committee, composed of faculty and black students appointed by the dean, be set up to review the black demands relating to the curriculum and to report its findings and recommendations to the Academic Policy Committee. In addition, the faculty suggested that two black students from the proposed committee serve as consultants to the Academic Policy Committee and that other steps be taken to establish better communications between black students and the faculty and administration.

Tuesday, March 11: At around 1 P.M., ten to fifteen black students, wearing African dress and beating drums, occupied the lounge of the admissions office. Signs had been placed around the union directing people to the new "black cultural center" in the administration building. President Upton asked the demonstrators to leave, since they were hindering rather than helping efforts to implement the black demands and, according to his policy, warned that civil authorities would be called and that the students were all liable to arrest unless they left. The students remained until 4:45 P.M., but police were not brought in.

Friday, March 14: Dean Kolb, as chairman of the faculty, issued a statement outlining the steps that had so far been taken in response to demands that directly concerned the faculty. Of prime importance was establishment of the recommended ad hoc committee composed of faculty and black students. Kolb said that the faculty, at its March 24 meeting, would consider whether this committee should be made permanent. (It was.) He added that members were being considered for the committee; the student members—drawn from a list of nominees submitted by the AAU—would also serve as his advisory committee. As committee members, he said, they would act on an individual basis rather than in a bloc "and should represent the range of individual opinion within [the AAU]." Moreover, some provision should be made by the ad hoc committee to represent the opinions of blacks who were not members of the AAU. In connection with Upton's suggestion that Beloit pioneer a videotape program relating to black studies, he said that plans had been made to tape the summer symposium, which was to deal with the concept of blackness.

Saturday, March 15: The Positive Action Committee (PAC), an organization composed chiefly of concerned white students, sponsored a number of activities for Parents' Day, including a craft sale and an art show, to raise funds, particulary for the high-potential education program but also for black scholarships and professorships.

Wednesday, March 26: The *Round Table* issued a "progress report" on what had been done in response to the black demands. Among the definite actions taken was establishment of the Faculty-Black Student Committee, which had so far planned the summer symposium, met with the common courses committees to consider inclusion of sections on blackness, and generally acted "as a 'clearing house' for communication between the Afro-American Union and academic departments and the faculty at large." The AAU was not yet satisfied, however, with concrete responses to its demands for more black studies and for a mandatory course on the concept of blackness.

Another positive step was the appointment of black students

to act as consultants to each department in reevaluating the curriculum "to include relevant contributions by black experts." A black special assistant to the dean of the college had been hired; he would serve chiefly as director of the high-potential education program but would also function as a black counselor and financial aid consultant, thus satisfying two of the black demands. A site had been selected for the cultural center, to be established at the college's expense. Other plans had been made (for instance, to hire two black recruiters, as an effort toward increasing the representation of blacks in the student body), and discussion among blacks and other groups was continuing.

Friday, March 28: Three black students—including Mike Young, president of the AAU—were indicted by the office of the dean of students for disruption of Professor Ruiz's lecture—part of the Cuban Convocation Cluster—on February 28. They were ordered to appear before the Judicial Board (J-Board).

Sunday, April 6, 2 P.M.: The Judicial Board meeting called to hear the case of the three black students had to be canceled because a quorum was lacking. Acting Chairman Robert Arnebeck rescheduled the hearing for Tuesday night, announcing that it would be open to the public. In protest of this decision, Dean of Students John Gwin walked out, and two members of J-Board resigned.

Monday, April 7: Arnebeck issued a statement explaining his actions of the previous evening and attacking the structure and procedures of J-Board: "We have no need for a group of six students to hear in private the complaints of the dean against fellow students. . . . I am personally proud of the number of fellow students I have tried to protect from the inane and unnecessary strictures Deans Gwin and Gilbertsen enforced upon their behavior. J-Board . . . can no longer be a 'deans court.' This means there can no longer be closed hearings. This means that the dean of students must adjust his attitude towards student regulations." Arnebeck also maintained that disruption of the Ruiz lecture has been "an action of orderly protest designed to correct the white bias that is probably as old as Beloit itself" and that therefore the charges against the three black students should be dropped. His statement was endorsed by the Associated Student Senate.

Tuesday, April 8: At 5 P.M., the Student Affairs Committee met to inform Dean Gwin that the two vacancies on J-Board had been filled. The committee also ruled "that the Student Regulations imply that all J-Board hearings are closed and that only after the hearing is completed can portions or all of the information concerning the case be released." They advised Gwin to take his case against Arnebeck to the student senate.

At the J-Board meeting that evening, it was decided that the case against the black students should be heard at once. Arnebeck disqualified himself from hearing the case. Gwin (who had not been formally notified of the meeting and was not present) declined, by telephone, to appear, saying that he was not fully prepared to present his case. Subsequently, J-Board voted to reconvene the following evening and expressed the feeling that a rule should be established giving both defendant and prosecutor twenty-four-hour notice of rescheduled hearings.

Wednesday, April 9, 7 P.M.: Because J-Board was once again short of a quorum, Acting Chairman Arnebeck requalified himself. Dean Gwin protested, indicating that if Arnebeck continued to sit on the case, the office of the dean of students would withdraw the case from consideration by J-Board and appeal it directly to the Student Affairs Committee. Between 7 and 9 P.M., a crowd of about sixty students "waited noisily" outside the hearing room. Meanwhile, one of the missing J-Board members had been located (he had had car trouble) and promised to get there as soon as possible.

At 8:30, Gwin declared that he would drop charges against the black students. According to an article in the *Round Table,* "the dean presumably did this for two reasons: he empathized with the black students and their inconvenience with the rescheduling problems of J-Board, and he expressed a concern for the future of J-Board and student responsibility in judicial affairs in general."

In a press conference following the meeting, the three black students criticized the structure and bias of J-Board. One said: "J-Board is what we are fighting against, against being judged by necessarily white standards of conduct, against being forced to conform to white western values that don't apply to us." Another said that Gwin and the faculty should realize "the fact of life—

that values are changing and that they should change too or accept the changing values."

Goals and Changes. The main goal of the protesters and their sympathizers was to bring about the changes specified in the twelve black demands. The rationale underlying the specific demands was stated broadly in an opening paragraph of the AAU statement: "The demands we have proposed will provide a cultural and educational vehicle for creating the awareness, confidence, and determination in black people that is necessary for any type of co-existence between black and white in this country." A subsidiary goal, which figured especially in the opening stages of the protest, was to open campus facilities to the townspeople, particularly black youth, and to draw them more closely into the life of the campus. The reform of the Judicial Board became a goal of some prominence toward the end of the protest.

The protest had a number of positive outcomes. In general, efforts were made by all parties to respond quickly and meaningfully to the black demands. There were several definite results. A Faculty-Black Student Committee was established, on a continuing basis, to work on implementing curricular changes mentioned in the black demands. A summer symposium on the concept of blackness was scheduled; it was to be videotaped, in view of the possibility that Beloit might pioneer a full series of videotaped black studies programs for use at other institutions. The proposal originated with President Upton. The university common courses committees, after meeting with black students, recommended a list of black readings for all sections. Members of the AAU were selected to serve as consultants to each department.

Black students were invited to meet with the Admissions Committee to discuss what steps might be taken to increase the enrollment of blacks at Beloit. It was decided to hire two black recruiters for the fall semester. A black special assistant to the dean of the college was hired to act as director of the high-potential education program and as counselor and financial aid consultant to black students.

The administration approved the notion of black students living together on a voluntary basis. A black cultural and social center was established, to be run by black students but to be open to all.

President Upton gave instructions that a judicial process be set up so that complaints against individual employees accused of harassing black students would be tried promptly "and with full justice provided both the accuser and the accused." Finally, the charges of disruption brought against three black students were dropped. No other disciplinary action was taken against the protesters.

Student Power Protest: American University

The protest at American University in the early part of 1969 had issues of both student power and student life.[2] Though the short-range issue was settled in a little over a week, repercussions were felt until the end of the semester in May.

Setting. Located in the District of Columbia, American University is noted for its School of Government and Public Information and its School of International Service. It also attracts large proportions of students who plan to go into business administration or law. It is a large, coeducational university, affiliated with the Methodist Church.

Of only moderate selectivity, American University enrolls students who are close to the national average in their high school records. Their degree aspirations are slightly higher than those of students nationally. In 1968, 62 percent planned to get post-baccalaureate degrees, compared to 49 percent of the national college population. American University students are a fairly affluent group, however, with 82 percent coming from families whose incomes are above $10,000 (compared to 51 percent nationally). Their parents' educational levels are also higher than the national average.

Student attitudes toward campus and social issues tend to be liberal except on the matter of giving preferential treatment in ad-

[2]The documenter of the American University protest was David A. Duty, editor-in-chief of the *Eagle* at the time of the protest. Except where otherwise noted, all information and all direct quotations were taken from articles in the *Eagle* or from an interview with Steve Behrens, a reporter who covered much of the protest and who took some notes that were not used in the newspaper articles.

missions to disadvantaged students; only 39 percent agreed that this should be done, compared to 55 percent of freshmen nationally in 1968. They were slightly more inclined to feel that the chief benefit of a college education is monetary (41 percent) than were students at the other case-study institutions (37 percent) but less inclined to agree with this statement than students nationally (58 percent). A fairly large number (27 percent, compared to 21 percent nationally) gave high priority to the life goal of becoming a community leader, but a relatively small proportion valued contributing to scientific theory (4 percent, compared to 11 percent nationally).

Issues. The immediate issue was whether an "inaugural gala" would be held on campus in honor of self-proclaimed United States "President-in-Exile" Dick Gregory, a black comedian with a flair for social and political satire. The incident that precipitated the protest was the refusal of the administration to grant permission for the use of university facilities for such a gala.

The greater issue—control of the decision-making process at American University—came to the fore almost immediately. The students questioned the right of the administration to determine what was "in the best educational interest of the entire academic community."

Cast of Characters. The Steering Committee was the leadership group responsible for planning actions and submitting proposals to the protesting students. While some existing organizations played a role in the protest, it was largely initiated and supported by non-radical white students, and it was they who elected the sixteen members to the Steering Committee, which was formed on the first day of the protest. Its chairman was Pap Secka, a graduate student from Gambia enrolled in the School of International Service and a student senator during his undergraduate career at the university. The Gregory affair was the first and only protest in which he played a role.

The Organization of Afro-American Students at the American University (OASATAU), a black student group composed of about forty persons, was one of the organizations that requested university facilities for the "inaugural gala." It also called the rally that opened the protest. Its president, Bert Coppock, played a small role in subsequent events. In the spring of 1968, OASATAU had been involved in a previous protest, when it demanded that the administration increase the number of black students and establish a black studies program.

The Student Association (SA) had little to do with the Gregory affair, though it passed a few motions supporting the protesters and offered legal counsel to any students who felt that their rights were being violated. The Student Senate, made up of twenty-four members elected each spring, was its legislative organ. Several individual officers of the SA executive board and the Student Senate played roles in the events, including President Luiz Simmons and Comptroller Robert Whitmore. Vice-President Walker J. (Moose) Foster can probably be regarded as the chief protest leader. He was also a member of OASATAU and was eventually elected to the Tripartite Committee described below.

The original decision that university facilities could not be used for the Gregory inaugural gala was made by Bernard Hodinko, vice-president for student life at American University. George Williams, who was serving his first year as president in 1968–1969 and had been described in the media as "reform-minded," played no part in the original decision but became deeply involved following a sit-in at his office; he was responsible for issuing all subsequent statements of administrative policy. Donald Dedrick, director of the physical plant, supported the negative decision.

The University Senate, a body composed of all full-time faculty members at the university, supported many of the protesters' actions. A former senate chairman, James Weaver, helped to mediate the dispute by drawing up a resolution. The university chapter of the American Association of University Professors voted in favor of use of the university facilities for the inaugural gala. Though a substantial number of the six hundred faculty members at American University were national AAUP members, only the 13 percent who had paid their dues to the local chapter could vote, according to Robert Blanchard, chapter president and a leader of faculty support of the protesters.

The campus chapter of Students for a Democratic Society (SDS)—which claimed about twenty-five members, a dozen of whom were hard-core activists—played a very minor role in the protest. Its members tried to take over the events by urging the students to more radical, arrest-provoking actions at several points.

One of its spokesmen was cochairman Jack Davis. The local chapter of Young Americans for Freedom (YAF), a national student conservative organization, was also small, having no more than twenty-five members. As a group, it claimed to take no action, but several members circulated petitions supporting the administration position.

A Tripartite Committee, recommended by the University Senate, grew out of the protest. Its membership was to consist of five administrators, five faculty members, two graduate students, and four undergraduates. Its chief function was to evaluate the current university government and recommend revisions.

Louis Loeb, an activist professor in the School of Government and Public Administration, was one of the chief faculty critics of the administration stand on the Gregory affair. Gary Weaver, a former assistant dean of the School of International Service, was one of the faculty members who originally suggested that Gregory hold his "inaugural gala" on campus; he supported the students in the protest. Charles Rother, the university Methodist chaplain, was another supporter of the student protesters.

Chronology of Events. Monday, February 24: Bernard Hodinko, university vice-president for student life, announced that the administration would not grant permission for an "inaugural ball" to be held on campus in honor of Dick Gregory. Gregory had spoken at American University on February 16 and was approached afterward by several students and faculty members who suggested the possibility of a ball to him; Gregory approved of the idea. The Student Association (SA) and the black student association (OASATAU) had filed a request to use Leonard Center (a gymnasium where concerts were occasionally given) and Clendenen Gymnasium (a women's gym used by the university theatre group for rehearsals and performances) for what they initially called a "dance" in Gregory's honor. The administration had granted permission. Later, the request was changed to indicate that the occasion was an "inaugural gala." Then the decision was reversed.

The basic reason for this reversal, according to Hodinko, was that university policy precluded the use of university facilities for nonstudent and non-education-oriented functions. Donald Dedrick, director of the physical plant, opposed granting permission on the grounds that "outside groups" should not be allowed to use university facilities.

At a meeting between Hodinko, Dedrick, SA President Luiz Simmons, OASATAU member Bert Coppock, Student Activities Director Terry Hohman, and SA Vice-President and OASATAU member Moose Foster, the administration explained that both gyms had already been reserved for the night of March 4 by the intramural athletic office and by the university theatre group. Therefore, neither would be available for the "gala" even if permission to hold it were granted; the Collier Room, a multipurpose room in Mary Graydon Center (the student union building), was available, however, if the students still wanted to hold the dance they had originally planned.

Foster reminded Dedrick that university facilities had been used by "outside groups" on two earlier occasions: by federal troops during Washington's urban disorders in April 1968 and by the Poor People's Campaign in May and June of that same year. According to Foster, Dedrick replied, "Moose, you've got me on that point." Hodinko later said that, in those two instances, permission had been granted by former President Hurst R. Anderson, who had retired in August; therefore, the precedent was not applicable to the current case.

In response to this negative decision, OASATAU called a student rally for the following day.

Tuesday, February 25, noon: The scheduled student rally was held on the steps of Mary Graydon Center. Moose Foster called the university a "lid on the black community" and criticized it for remaining "untouched by" that community. On the specific issue, he told the four hundred or so students at the rally that precedent existed for Gregory's use of campus facilities (referring to the use of facilities by federal troops and the Poor People's Campaign).

Foster urged his audience to "think of the real issues." He then asked if they were ready to "fill the president's office" and present him with their demands. The main demand was, of course, that permission be granted for the inaugural gala. But a more fundamental issue had developed; it was "arbitrary decision-making policy on the part of the AU administration, without consideration of student desires." An editorial in the *Eagle* that day called the decision by the administration a "regrettable denial."

Tuesday, February 24, 12:30 P.M.: About two hundred students responded to Foster's appeal and followed him and other emerging protest leaders (most of them black students) to the administration building across campus. When they arrived, at about 12:30 P.M., most of the staff in the building, including the president, were out to lunch. When the protesters learned this they went inside to wait. About seventy-five students and some faculty members crowded into the president's office.

Returning from lunch at about 12:45, President George Williams found his office packed with standing and sitting students. The *Eagle,* describing the situation as a "tense, but peaceful and orderly session," said that the president appeared "obviously shaken" by the number of students in his office. He asked them to leave, promising to talk with Foster and other designated representatives if they would do so, but the students refused.

The following transcript of what occurred at the session is taken from a student reporter's notes:

WILLIAMS: This university is not going to be operated . . . in a situation where a large body of people participate in a discussion of a situation in which I have been completely open.

FOSTER: Every person would like to see what goes on here. I'm at a loss to explain university policy to all these people.

SDS MEMBERS: We want Dick Gregory here, and we don't see any reason why he can't be here.

WILLIAMS: The decision stands. It has not been changed, and it will not be changed. And it is not going to be changed by threat of force or a sit-in.

FOSTER: Our terms are not violent. We want a human being on this campus. We won't be drawn by your plastic smile.

WILLIAMS: The proposed gala is not in furtherance of the educational mission of this university. You may disagree, but it is my position to make that decision. It will not change like this.

FOSTER: This university is racist. We feel that Dick Gregory is important to the nation. We're talking about hunger right here in Washington. What if my people were to eat up everything in sight, . . . to become human locusts? This time they might come up past Connecticut Avenue.

WILLIAMS: But decisions like this are not made at a a rally. I've heard what you have to say. This meeting is concluded. I ask you all to leave. . . . The decision stands.

FOSTER: This is not the end. This is not defeat. The next level is confrontation.

WILLIAMS: I hope it will not come to that.

The students left without further comment, adjourning to a classroom where they elected a sixteen-member Steering Committee to be responsible for planning subsequent events and for submitting proposals to larger student groups for approval. Pap Secka was elected chairman and later became one of the principal spokesmen for the protesting students.

Tuesday, February 25, 6 P.M.: At a press conference, the Steering Committee announced its plans for Wednesday, which included a 10 A.M. meeting with President Williams for "reconsideration" of the issue. The meeting had been arranged by SA Comptroller Robert Whitmore. The committee stated that it would seek a reply from Williams by noon Wednesday.

Pap Secka said at the press conference: "We do not believe President Williams can reflect the educational goals of the entire community." A petition asking for reconsideration of the issue was circulated until it was announced that Williams had agreed to the next day's meeting.

Jack Seigle, a professor in the Department of Communication, predicted that the faculty would support the protesting students. Several fraternities said they would cancel their intramural basketball tournament scheduled for March 4, if the decision on the gala was reversed. (Dedrick had referred to their reservation of Leonard Center at the Monday meeting.)

Wednesday, February 26, 10 A.M.: The events of the day began with the meeting between President Williams and ten students—four members of the Steering Committee, four student senators, and two members of both bodies. At the meeting, the issue was heatedly debated for nearly an hour. Williams told the students he would reply by 5 P.M.

Nearly five hundred students gathered at Mary Graydon Center at 11 A.M. to learn the results of the meeting. Moose Foster asked the students to walk to the lawn of the president's building to show their "appreciation" to Williams for agreeing to reconsider the decision. He spelled out "a-p-p-r-e-c-i-a-t-i-o-n" for the benefit of the Washington press who, he said, had "mangled" reports of the AU situation.

The crowd walked across campus to the president's building, but there was no reply to their gesture. Noon passed, and the crowd dispersed until the next scheduled rally at 2 P.M.

Meanwhile, the university chapter of the American Association of University Professors had met and voted to support the Gregory inaugural gala.

Wednesday, February 26, 2 P.M.: The reply from President Williams had not arrived by the noon deadline set by the Steering Committee the previous day, although the students knew that Williams had said he would reply by 5 P.M. At the afternoon rally, the protesters decided to sit in at various campus buildings for short periods of time and then move on to other buildings, particularly if the police came.

About two hundred students filled the vaulted two-story lobby of the neighboring McKinley Building and sat on the wide steps, as Steering Committee Chairman Secka emphasized that classes should not be disrupted. Staff members in the College of Continuing Education (CCE) offices went about their work as Jack Davis, cochairman of SDS, "educated" the students on the extensive police-training program conducted by CCE. The building (named for President McKinley) is known as the birthplace of chemical warfare research, and Davis made a point of that fact.

After twenty or thirty minutes, the students decided to move on to the Asbury Administration Building, where the office of admissions, the registrar's office, the central offices of the department of languages, and several classrooms are located. They filled the courtyard and main stairways and overflowed onto the roof of the building. Members of OASATAU, acting as "marshals," herded jubilant students off the roof, explaining that their presence there was a violation of District of Columbia law. Television film crews rushed around, attempting to keep up with the fast-moving crowd.

Wednesday, February 26, 4 P.M.: Following a meeting with top-level administrators and deans, President Williams released a statement reaffirming the negative decision on the gala. He said that "a one-shot affair . . . no matter how commendable or worthy its sponsors, its motivation, or its purpose, will not advance effective consideration of the [social problems that face our community]. . . . I propose to those with a serious interest in relating this university to the community that they set about devising a serious program of community involvement drawing on the strengths of the university rather than merely on some of its already overtaxed physical facilities."

At about the same time that this statement was released, the students left the Asbury Building and marched to the Ward Circle Building. Gathered in one of the large lecture rooms, they laughed as Pap Secka read Williams's statement aloud.

Black and white students, some with walkie-talkies and others with brooms, acted as "security guards" in the Ward Circle Building. The lecture hall was filled, standing room and aisles included: some six hundred students were present. After a first round of talks by Steering Committee members and by several faculty members, Chairman Secka confronted the students with the eventual choice: to leave when the anticipated court injunction was delivered; or to stay and risk violence with District of Columbia or other law enforcement officers. Two viewpoints on the question emerged. Most of the crowd, led by the black students, were in favor of withdrawing from the building when the time came and regrouping later. A few, led by SDS Cochairman Jack Davis, wanted to stay, although another SDS member, John Crouch, spoke for withdrawal.

In an emotional address, Secka said that he would not preside over a divided Steering Committee or a divided group of students. What the Steering Committee and the students gathered there decided by vote, everyone must do, he said. Otherwise, the ranks would be "divided and conquered." After a hefty voice vote in favor of the withdrawal tactic, Davis and others said they would abide by the decision.

Robert Whitmore, SA comptroller, backed the protesting students with a pledge of financial aid in case of arrests and suggested that the SA pay the ballroom charges at the Hotel America, where the Gregory gala had been rescheduled. At 8:30 P.M., the SA Finance Committee met and voted to back Whitmore's pledges, though final approval was delayed until the regular Student Senate meeting at noon on Friday.

Jane Silberman, representing Dick Gregory, said she was glad that the question of his gala site had been a catalyst for the protest. She and others reported that Gregory would be returning to the campus that night to speak to the students.

Tom Reeves, an instructor in the School of International Service, called Williams's refusal to okay the Gregory gala "stupid" because of the widespread student support of the issue. "I believe the president has hoped to provoke extreme action" that would lead more conservative students to react and thereby "seem to corroborate the president's act." He concluded, "I hope your political responsibility is not a flash in the pan, but instead turns into self-government of the university."

Former Assistant Dean Gary Weaver of the School of International Service, another young and popular professor, said he was "tremendously disappointed" in Williams's failure to change his mind. Weaver said he had told Williams that, if students were arrested, some members of the faculty would go too.

Professor Louis Loeb of the School of Government and Public Administration asked that the gathering stick together for at least two days so they could arrange discussion sections and seminars in the newly proclaimed "New American University." The Gregory case, Loeb said, was a "classic example of arbitrary decision-making." The issue was not the process that Williams followed, he added, "but the people he had to talk to before making the final decision. Who is he going to listen to?"

Chaplain Charles Rother said of the Gregory incident: "This is the most beautiful thing that has happened to American University." He recalled the tears that had come to his eyes when Williams had spoken of AU and its city in his inaugural address in October. "I thought here was a man who sees where it is; well, I was fooled." At various times during the protest, Rother and other speakers referred to the president's inaugural remarks, in which he called on American University to "partake of its environment" in the Washington community. They accused Williams of hypocrisy when he denied permission for the Gregory gala.

As Rother urged the students to come over to the Kay Spiritual Life Center to "pray about it," Williams was again meeting with key administrators to determine what action to take next. It was decided to seek a temporary restraining order or an injunction against the students who had announced they would stay in the building all night.

When the students learned that the injunction would definitely be served, they withdrew from the building, leaving behind reams of paper—programs and publicity material for the "New AU." District marshals arrived on campus with the temporary restraining order, but finding no one around to serve with it they left.

Thursday, February 27: With the establishment of the New AU in the Ward Circle Building, the protesting students were less inclined to use the steps of the Mary Graydon Center as their meeting and rallying place. Instead they gathered in the lecture hall, organizing and planning future strategies.

President Williams issued a statement at 1 P.M., announcing that he was lifting the restraining order (which had never been served) as "a demonstration of my confidence in the faculty and students." In the statement, Williams also said: "In making this decision, I was impressed with the earnest assurances of a cross-section of faculty and student leaders that members of this community will pursue a course of reasonable discussion and orderly procedure in the consideration of the vital matters which affect each of us."

The University (faculty) Senate met, as scheduled, at 3 P.M. After first expressing support of the use of the Ward Circle Building by protesting students and faculty members, the senate considered a motion drawn up by former Senate Chairman James Weaver and SA President Luiz Simmons to establish two university committees to consider the issues. One would reevaluate present university governance and recommend revisions. It was to have sixteen members: five administrators, five faculty members, four undergraduate students, and two graduate students. This committee, which came to be known as the Tripartite Committee, played an important role in the attempted resolution of the Gregory affair and the deeper question of decision-making at American University. The second proposed committee was to draw up guidelines for the use of campus facilities and to create new procedures for deciding who would use them. (The Student Senate, meeting in caucus earlier, had passed a resolution approving the two committees, but final action was delayed until its regular session on Friday.)

Before the University Senate considered the motion, President Williams addressed it, making his first public comment on the issue since it had erupted. Williams said that the time had come "to take inventory" of the university's current decision-making processes and "to build on the highly constructive foundation that has been set through conversations this week." He continued: "We are working together. If there is anything this university has learned this week, it's that dissent, challenge, and opinions can result in growth and improvement for all of us. . . . What we need is an inventory and a reexamination of how decisions are reached. We're at the point where the decision must be made. . . . It's time we began solving, not talking." Williams concluded his fifteen-minute impromptu speech by commending what he called "the responsible goodwill and involvement of the students and faculty members" in the Gregory controversy. On that note, the president left the senate to its business. The resolution establishing the two committees passed unanimously.

Meanwhile, several members of the campus chapter of Young Americans for Freedom (YAF) were attempting, unsuccessfully, to obtain another restraining order that would prohibit the "unlawful entry and occupation of the Ward Circle Building." One member of YAF explained that the action was not an organizational action but rather the individual effort of several "concerned" students who wanted "to prevent further riots on campus."

With the establishment of the Tripartite Committee, the students who were still in the Ward Circle Building began to drift apart on the question of what to do next. Some felt that further action should be taken, since the Gregory issue had still not been decided favorably. Others said the New AU should adopt a wait-and-see attitude.

Thursday, February 27, 7 P.M.: As the uncertainty continued, and as most students lingered around the lecture hall to see what was going to happen next, President Williams issued another statement saying that a dance—not an inaugural gala—could be held on the campus. "Consideration will be given to a request for a student-sponsored dance in a suitable facility for AU students and their guests, at which Mr. Dick Gregory might appear."

Many of the protesting students viewed this statement as a capitulation on the part of the administration and a victory for the protesters. Actually, it was no more than a restatement of the original decision that the dance could take place on campus. With the release of this statement and an announcement by the Interfraternity Council that it would relinquish the needed facilities on the night of March 4, the tension that had been building during the week seemed to dissipate. A rock-and-roll group that had donated its time to the New AU planned to remain in the building throughout the night.

The easing of the situation brought dissension among the protesting students about their next course of action. In an interview with an *Eagle* reporter, Pap Secka remarked: "It's not really significant that we have dissension. The miracle of the whole thing is that we got together in the first place. . . . The removal of the visible opposition always calls for reorientation. The larger the group, the longer it takes, and the harder it is to change the course of the entire group." He explained that the group was in the process of analyzing where it had come and where it was going. "We must begin a very serious and intensive study of the questions we've raised."

As Secka spoke, members of the New AU security and cleanup committees kept busy at their respective jobs. Reports of outsiders coming onto campus to incite further student action were soon proved false.

At about 8 P.M., Williams issued another statement, calling for a joint session of the University Senate and the Student Senate on Wednesday, March 5, at which he would submit his "specific recommendations for action in various areas which affect academic and student life on this campus."

Friday, February 28: The Student Senate met at 12:30 P.M. and gave its formal approval to the Tripartite Committee. It was understood that the undergraduate members on the committee would be elected under procedures set forth by the SA election committee.

For the New AU, it was a day of rest, although scheduled committee sessions continued throughout the day. For President Williams, it was the first regular workday of the week since the Gregory affair had become an issue.

The Council of Graduate Students announced that it would meet the following Tuesday to decide whether it would participate in the student election of members to the Tripartite Committee.

Saturday, March 1–Sunday, March 2: Final plans were made for the election of undergraduates to the Tripartite Committee. It was announced that nominations would be held on Tuesday.

The New AU committees met during the weekend and issued a series of tentative proposals for the Tripartite Committee to discuss. They dealt with such matters as student life, curriculum reform, the university and the District of Columbia community, the university and the federal government, and the decision-making process. A joint committee on departmental decision-making and student–faculty relations was also proposed. Finally, a general assembly of the New AU was announced for 6 P.M. Monday.

Monday, March 3: Although the administration made no formal announcement on the subject, plans progressed for a concert and dance to be held "in Gregory's honor" on Tuesday, March 4. The fraternities that would have played intramural basketball in Leonard Center that night had agreed to relinquish the gymnasium. Dick Gregory announced that he would return to the campus for the concerts and the dance, though his "inaugural gala" would be at the Hotel America in downtown Washington.

In a speech at the Monday session of the New AU, Pap Secka raised the question of whether the New AU would take part in the Tripartite Committee, a point on which there had been some doubt. Secka announced that the Steering Committee had voted to "play the game within the existing rules of the game," that is, to participate in the committee. The resolution finally adopted by the general assembly of the New AU included a section giving the New AU the right to recall any student who "failed to follow the objectives" of that group; thus, the group would have some assurance that participation on the Tripartite Committee would not hurt its cause. Following this decision, the New AU elected a slate of four undergraduates (one being Moose Foster) and two graduate students (one being Pap Secka) for nomination on Tuesday.

Tuesday, March 4: President Williams, addressing the joint session of the senates, called for consideration of a long list of academic and other university reforms. Among the possible changes were abolishment of general university requirements; elimination of the foreign language requirement for all students in the College of Arts and Sciences; a grant of academic credit for internships and off-campus work, as well as for work on student government and publication staffs; establishment of pass–fail grading in most, if not all, courses; reduction of course requirements for majors in specific fields and for graduation; and selection of courses by the individual student based "not on compulsion but on attractiveness and improved counseling."

The president emphasized throughout that he was merely making suggestions for consideration by the existing committees and legislatives bodies within the university. "There is nothing sacred about the present university structure, organization, or personnel," Williams said. The three general areas he touched on were university governance and organization, the quality of education and its processes, and student life at the university.

Williams said that the confusion and turmoil surrounding the Gregory affair resulted from a "lack of understanding . . . of the functions of students, faculty, administrators, and trustees." He attributed that lack of understanding to the fact that "layers of responsibility [had been] assigned over the years to each group" and suggested that the University Senate, the Student Senate, and other decision-making bodies reevaluate their roles.

The president blamed "rapidly changing technology, rapid growth of the university, and social pressures" for most of the existing curriculum problems. "The curricula of this university are generally inadequate to meet the needs of students and of the world in which they now live and in which they will lead," he said. "I fail to see merit in a rigid structure built of lock-step, three-credit-hour courses, particularly when we believe that education also occurs outside the classroom." He called for a reevaluation of faculty tenure policies and suggested a six-year term for faculty members, after which their work would be reviewed by their faculty colleagues, students, and possibly administrators.

Regarding student life, Williams mentioned the shortcomings of the residence, dining, medical, and guidance facilities; each of these student services, he felt, could be improved after evaluation.

Though the President received a standing ovation at the conclusion of his thirty-minute speech, his critics immediately said that he had failed to discuss the "big question"—who was going to make the decisions and formulate the policies that affected the entire university community. Professor Loeb said the president fell "far short" of answering that question.

After Williams's speech, the action moved to the steps of Mary Graydon Center, where nominations for student members to the Tripartite Committee took place. The four undergraduate candidates on the New AU slate were formally nominated, along with six other independent and SA-backed candidates.

The Council of Graduate Students, after deciding to participate on the Tripartite Committee, organized and sponsored graduate student nominations and elections. Six graduate students were nominated, including the two New AU nominees, Pap Secka and Alex Ajay.

Elections among the faculty began on Tuesday and continued till the end of the week.

Tuesday, March 4: Dick Gregory returned to the campus on the night of his inauguration as United States president-in-exile. Plans for two concerts were altered so that one continuous concert and a dance were held at the same time that night. The concert took place in the Leonard Center, the dance in the Collier Room of Mary Graydon Center.

About eight hundred students and guests heard Gregory joke that he was actually the one responsible for getting permission for the concert and dance. He said he had sent President Williams a telegram informing him that Stokely Carmichael had been appointed "minister of education" of the administration-in-exile and that Carmichael would "wipe you [Williams] out" if permission for Gregory's appearance on campus was not granted.

Gregory urged the students to "convince the other fellow in

the White House that he's not the one." The students laughed and applauded as they indulged in what Pap Secka called "celebration of a partial victory." Echoing a speech he had delivered on campus about two weeks earlier, Gregory said "the most morally dedicated force in the history of America is you young folks." He told the students that whenever they went to jail "for right, then the jail becomes the prisoner."

Gregory's appearance signified the end of the specific issue that had arisen on Monday, February 24. The students had demanded that an "inaugural gala" be held on the campus. In one sense, that demand was met even before the controversy began, since the administration had granted permission for a dance of the kind that was finally held.

Thursday, March 20: The greater issue of decision-making within the university still remained. That was left in the hands of the Tripartite Committee. The four New AU undergraduate nominees were elected in the student elections. The two New AU nominees on the graduate student slate were soundly defeated by two more conservative students. The faculty elected its representatives, and President Williams appointed the administrators to the committee.

The committee held its first session on Thursday, March 20, and began to lay the groundwork, particularly with respect to procedures and scheduling of future meetings.

After nine meetings and about thirty-five hours of discussion, the Tripartite Committee accepted a report drawn up by its Resolutions Committee. It called for a minimum of one-third student representation on all committees of the whole in each teaching unit (school, college, and department).

Wednesday, May 28, and after: The Tripartite Committee proposal was sent to the University Senate for approval. The senate substituted an amendment calling for "meaningful student voting participation" (not one-third) on all teaching-unit committees. This decision was binding, since the Tripartite Committee had been created by a University Senate resolution. There was no student reaction to the senate's decision. Most students were beginning final examinations for a semester that had been exhausting, academically and otherwise.

Goals and Changes. The immediate goal of the protesting students and faculty members was to reverse the refusal by the administration to permit a Dick Gregory inaugural gala on campus. Their longer range goal was a restructuring of the university's decision-making process so that students would be given voting participation on all university committees.

The primary outcome of the Gregory affair was that on March 4 a dance was held on campus in honor of Gregory. Since such a dance had originally been approved by the administration, this represented no particular victory for the protesters, although many of them chose to regard it as one.

On the deeper issue of university decision-making procedures, the protesters also won less than they had hoped. Although the Tripartite Committee had specifically recommended that students be given one-third voting representation on all university committees, the University Senate revised this to a much vaguer stipulation of "meaningful" voting representation for students.

Antiwar Protest: Stanford University

One distinctive feature of the protest at Stanford University in the spring of 1969 was that it involved large numbers of people— both pro and con—who felt the issues deeply.[3] "Apathy" is certainly not an appropriate word to apply to the attitudes of the campus community in this instance. Not only the issues but also the protest events themselves were complex. Many organizations and persons at various points on the political spectrum played some role. The protest was supported by nonradical as well as radical groups; it encompassed all segments of the university and reached out to the community beyond the campus. Other characteristics were the occupation of buildings (on two occasions); strong counterprotest activity; the threat of and actual suspension of students; marches, rallies, and petitions; a boycott of classes; the seeking of an injunction; the calling in of civil police on several occasions; discussions and nego-

[3] The documenter of the Stanford protest was Marjorie Lozoff, research associate at Stanford. Except where otherwise noted in the text, all information and direct quotations were taken from articles in the *Stanford Daily* (the student newspaper), the *Stanford Observer* (a monthly tabloid published by the university), or the *Stanford News Service.*

tiations; the formation of committees to study the problem; and changes, though not necessarily those sought by the protesters.

Setting. Stanford University is a large, private, nonsectarian, coeducational institution located in the Palo Alto area of northern California. One of the most selective universities in the country, it recruits highly able students: of the 1968 classes, 92 percent made grades of B-plus or better in high school (compared to a mean of 60 percent for all the case study institutions and only 29 percent for institutions across the nation). Some 52 percent had received recognition in the National Merit competition (compared to 24 percent for the case study institutions on the average and 7 percent for institutions across the country). Understandably, the degree aspirations of these students tend to be high: in 1968, 84 percent planned to get graduate degrees (master's, doctoral, or professional), compared to 49 percent of freshmen across the nation. In addition, a higher-than-average proportion of Stanford students majored in "entrepreneurial" fields such as journalism, political science, history, business administration, and advertising. A somewhat lower-than-average proportion majored in such fields as fine arts, English, languages, speech, and music.

Stanford students tend to come from affluent backgrounds and to have very highly educated parents. In 1968, 83 percent of the students' fathers had at least some college (compared to a mean of 69 percent of the fathers of students at all the case study institutions and 42 percent of the fathers of students across the nation); 76 percent of the mothers had some college experience (compared to 61 percent for the case study institutions and 35 percent nationally).

In their attitudes toward social and campus issues, Stanford students may be characterized as more liberal than the average college student (as were students at most of the case study institutions), though they were somewhat less inclined to feel that students should have a major role in specifying the curriculum. Only 5 percent felt that the institution should have control over the off-campus behavior of students (compared to 23 percent of freshmen in general and 15 percent of freshmen at all the case study institutions), whereas about half agreed that disadvantaged students should be given preferential treatment in admissions (compared to 42 percent both nationally and at the case study institutions), and relatively few felt that college officials had been too lax in dealing with campus protest. They place an unusually high emphasis on the goal of helping others in difficulty. Comparatively few believed that the chief benefit of a college education was that it increased one's earning power, and few gave high priority to the goal of being financially prosperous.

Stanford had experienced considerable campus unrest before the protest described here. Protests over both racial issues and student power issues had taken place. One recurrent theme of student discontent was the composition of the board of trustees, which its critics viewed as dominated by business interests that had close ties with "war-dependent" industries. Many members of the Stanford community were deeply concerned about the university's involvement in defense-related research. The spring 1969 protest grew out of this concern and, more particularly, out of a protest that had occurred during the previous academic year directed chiefly by Students for a Democratic Society.

Issues. One of the major issues in the spring of 1969 protest at Stanford was the legitimacy of university engagement in war-related research. This issue gave impetus to the April 3d Movement (described below) and thus to the demonstrations. At one end of the continuum were those who wanted all such research stopped. They spoke out specifically against chemical, biological, and radiological warfare research; counterinsurgency research at home and abroad; research related to wars in Southeast Asia; and all classified research. At the other end of the continuum were the officials at Stanford Research Institute (SRI), who regarded defense research as a public service. The faculty came out in favor of the "openness" of research as an academic standard. The administration seemed to agree with the protesters, at least to the extent of saying that too much emphasis was being placed on military research and that there should be a gradual shift in the direction of more humane research projects.

Closely related was the issue of the academic freedom of the researcher. One student contrasted the right of researchers to do research and the right of the peoples of the world to live. On the other hand, the chairman of the Committee on Research Policy said: "Stanford has strict policies related to classified research and the committee makes a sharp distinction between the interests of the researcher and his work and the interests of the sponsor; we lean toward the researcher. . . . Institutions shouldn't try to coerce individuals. There's a difference between institutional and individual neutrality. . . . The individual investigator keeps his morality because he has the right to refuse to do research, but it is absolutely immoral to have a collective judgment made that he can't pursue research."

Many people expressed concern over interference with the rights of the individual researcher. William Rambo, director of the Stanford Electronics Laboratories, was disturbed by what would happen to his staff—particularly the graduate students—if there were a cut in the amount of defense research at SRI. The president of SRI, Charles Anderson, said that the scientific and professional staff would walk out if "some outside morals committee is set up to tell them what is and what is not morally acceptable in the search for knowledge." He added that SRI had internal guidance on research policy and that "as to research in support of national security, we feel that we have a nationwide morals committee of voters who elect representatives to decide what is and what is not needed for the common good."

A third issue growing out of the first two centered on the future of SRI. The protesting groups felt that the university should impose much closer controls on the institute. A poll, reported in the *Stanford Observer* of June 1969, showed that, of the SRI staff, 72 percent favored independence from the university and 81 percent rejected the idea of non-SRI people helping to determine research policy. The same poll showed that 68 percent of the students and 36 percent of the faculty wanted to bring SRI under closer control and felt that there should be a community committee to redirect SRI research activities. In favor of selling SRI were 18 percent of the students and 53 percent of the faculty. The view of the board of trustees was that SRI should be sold, and the president of the institute approved of this decision.

Another major issue was the composition of the board of trustees and its lack of responsiveness to student demands. Students involved in the protest movement felt the board was closely linked to the military-industrial complex and therefore had special interests in war-related research. Fred Cohen, writing in the May 6, 1969, edition of the *Stanford Daily,* contended that the trustees' "positions have been shaped by occupying seats at the acme of the corporate hierarchy and eating too many meals at exclusive clubs. All of them, liberals and conservatives, firmly believe in the national security state and the global hegemony of the American multinational corporations." In particular, students were angered by the slowness of the board to respond to their demands and by the failure of its members to inform the Stanford community of their positions on the subject of SRI.

A secondary issue arising out of the protest itself—and one of the sorest points—was the legitimacy of the tactics used by the protesters—namely, the occupation of buildings on two occasions. The first sit-in, at the Applied Electronics Laboratory, received considerably more support, from both students and faculty members, though some expressed disapproval of the technique of disruption and interference with laboratory employees. The second sit-in was regarded with some disfavor even by those involved in or sympathetic with the protest, probably because, as one student said, it was brought about by a "manipulated" decision. Moreover, it involved some violence and property damage.

From the first, the administration deplored the disruptive tactics used and maintained that the protesters were violating "established procedures and obligations." For instance, Provost Lyman said: "At some point, defenses must be invoked against wanton, indiscriminate, and arbitrary action designed to force university acquiescence in the views of any campus groups, no matter how high-minded."

One student defended the first sit-in on three grounds: no disruption of a university activity had occurred because war-related research "is not a proper university function or approved activity"; legal means of protest had proved ineffective; and conflicting rights have a relative importance. "The university policy sets up a 'balancing test' between rights—the rights to continue research, both war-related and other kinds; the rights of those affected by such research; the rights of students who haven't gotten effective action."

The response to the protest was another secondary issue. Many writers praised the administration for its combination of firmness and restraint in dealing with the protesters and its willingness to consult with faculty before taking any action. Others criticized specific steps taken. One writer, for instance, felt that, by the use of an injunction, "the administration admitted that the internal governing structure at Stanford is unable to handle the crisis on campus." An injunction was, in this view, a threat to the peace "and brings Stanford closer to losing control of its own destiny." Though the Academic Senate supported the president's actions, some faculty members objected to the suspension of students, viewing this as an interference "with the traditional autonomy of instructors to decide who shall be allowed to audit" classes. The Stanford Judicial Council also supported the president's actions, except for two dissenting students who felt that he violated due process by imposing sanctions on students without a prior hearing. Finally, there were those who felt that the president had not gone far enough. Governor Ronald Reagan said of the sit-in at the Applied Electronics Laboratory: "I think the administration should do what they did at Harvard and go in there and get them out. . . . The protest involves an infringement on the rights of others who are paying tuition to go to that school as well as those teaching and doing research."

Cast of Characters. Stanford Research Institute (SRI), a contract research organization in the applied sciences, was the focus of the controversy. At the beginning of the protest, it was connected with Stanford University, though its president, Charles Anderson, was answerable neither to the university nor to the board of trustees but rather to a forty-member SRI board of directors elected by the trustees, many of whom were members. Weldon B. Gibson, executive vice-president, defined its purpose as follows: "Within our capabilities and research fields, the institute attempts to serve our government and allies as best we can." He pointed out that, in addition to the defense research that was the cause of the agitation, SRI did research on "projects of social concern." One division of SRI, the Electronics Laboratories, conducted about $600,000 worth of classified electronics research per year. Its director was William Rambo.

The April 3d Movement (A3M), an ad hoc group that initiated the protest, consisted initially of around eight hundred members of the Stanford–Palo Alto community who wanted SRI to stop all war-related research and refuse further war contracts. The group was responsible for most of the protest demonstrations. Its size varied; as incidents became more severe and A3M more radical, supporters dropped out. The university chapter of Students for a Democratic Society (SDS) had played a leadership role in previous protests against SRI. Many members of this left-wing group joined the A3M.

The Stanford–SRI Coalition, whose existence antedated A3M, consisted of faculty members, students, and citizens opposed to war-related research at SRI. It took no active part in the demonstrations. The Concerned Faculty for SRI was a group of fifty faculty members who supported the protest but urged moderation.

Since the Stanford protest was directed chiefly at matters under the control of the board of trustees, the administration played a relatively neutral role and was chiefly involved in dealing with demonstrations. Kenneth Pitzer, who assumed the office of president in the fall of 1968, was generally sympathetic with the protesters and agreed that national priorities should be adjusted. At the same time he was determined that due process should be observed, in accordance with procedures established by the Campus Disruption Policy, and he acted firmly against disruptive tactics. Richard W. Lyman, provost and vice-president, shared Pitzer's views. Another key administrative figure was Joel Smith, dean of students.

The twenty-three-member board of trustees was regarded as "the enemy" by many protesters and was chiefly responsible for both touching off and ending the protest. The trustees were general members of the SRI Corporation and elected the SRI board of directors. President of the trustees was W. Parmer Fuller III. During the protest, a special committee, headed by John Gardner, was appointed to study and make recommendations about the board's structure, composition, and functions.

The ad hoc University Committee on Research Policy, appointed in October 1968, consisted of students and faculty members assigned the task of studying the relationship between the university and SRI. Its chairman was William F. Baxter, professor of law. A Faculty Consultative Group on Campus Disruptions, appointed in the fall of 1968 by the Academic Senate at the request of the president, conferred frequently with the president throughout the period of protest.

The Stanford Judicial Council, a seven-member student-faculty group established in the fall of 1968, was considered the "key organ in the imposition of internal sanctions" and in determining whether members of the university community had violated campus policies on disruption. The Academic Council, a 999-member faculty body, supported the administrative handling of the protest. The Academic Senate began operations in the fall of 1968 as an ongoing deliberative body of fifty-three members who could deal with the day-to-day problems of the university. Meeting frequently throughout the period, it gave extensive attention to the protest. Its chairman was Leonard Schiff, professor of physics.

The Associated Students of Stanford University (ASSU), the student body organization, endorsed the protest and sponsored a Day of Concern. President Denis Hayes was an active moderating influence during the protest.

The Stanford chapter of the conservative Young Americans for Freedom (YAF) was active in opposing the protest. The Coalition for an Academic Community (CAC) was also active against the protest. At first its membership was drawn from the "Community of the Right," but later it claimed to have broadened its base of support to include some two hundred persons who opposed coercive tactics.

Chronology of Events. A number of events in late 1968 must be described briefly in order to understand the April 3d Movement fully. First, the Academic Senate had endorsed a new campus policy on disruptions. It then named a Faculty Consultative Group on Campus Disruptions. In addition, the University Committee on Research Policy had been informed to investigate the Stanford Research Institute (SRI) and its connection with the university and to report its findings in six months. Early in March 1969, the minority members of this committee reported that they were dissatisfied with the outcome of the study. Someone leaked the information that Stanford might sell SRI and thereby lose control of its activities.

In January 1969, twenty-nine members of SDS had disrupted a meeting of the board of trustees. In March, the newly operant Stanford Judicial Council found them guilty; this decision was regarded as the first important test of SJC, a "reform" judicial body consisting of both students and faculty members. (The former judiciary had included faculty members only.)

Tuesday, March 11: Five members of the board of trustees held a panel discussion attended by about a thousand members of the Stanford community. Student panelist David Pugh, a member of sds and later of the a3m, tried to elicit the trustees' attitudes toward sri, but they refused to express them pending the report of the University Committee on Research Policy (due April 15).

Friday, March 14: The Stanford–sri Coalition distributed a statement protesting research done at sri. It read, in part:

> A university committee is presently studying the relationship between Stanford and the Stanford Research Institute. We are disturbed to discover that in the course of the committee's deliberations, sri has renewed its major counterinsurgency project in Southeast Asia. In addition, two chemical-biological warfare contracts are pending. Furthermore, there is a danger that the study committee will recommend that the university sever ties with sri, thus absolving the university of responsibility for the work of the institute.
>
> As concerned members of the Stanford community, we feel that sri should direct its work toward creative and humane goals, and that the university community has a responsibility to make moral judgments. Specifically, we feel that under these standards, work in such areas as chemical-biological warfare and counterinsurgency in Asia and Latin America is unacceptable.

Thursday, April 3: Eight hundred members of the Palo Alto–Stanford community met to call for an immediate cessation of research on war-related projects and for rejection of all such research in the future. This group became known as the April 3d Movement (a3m) and was the dominant force in the protest.

Tuesday, April 8: The Stanford Board of Trustees asked the sri directors to impose a moratorium on any chemical and biological warfare contracts, pending the outcome of a reappraisal of ties between sri and the university.

Wednesday, April 9: Dissatisfied with the trustees' decision, nine hundred students met in Dinkelspiel Auditorium for three hours of discussion and debate. President Kenneth Pitzer was applauded when he told the crowd, "I hope your commitment to peace extends to this campus." After voting that the response of the board of trustees was "unacceptable," however, the students agreed by a two-to-one majority in a show of hands to stage a sit-in. The student body president, Denis Hayes, and several faculty members questioned this tactic, but Hayes said he would support the vote. About four hundred students than marched to the Applied Electronics Laboratory (AEL), filling it to capacity. Their purpose was to prevent classified research activities from continuing there. They agreed to leave classified materials untouched and not to destroy any property in the building.

Thursday, April 10: President Pitzer sent written notice to the protesters that they were violating university policies by preventing the normal conduct of business at AEL. He commented: "While I understand your deep commitment to bring change at the university and in this country, you are still not exempt from the ordinary obligations of all members of the Stanford community. I ask you to leave AEL and join me and other members of the community in working to resolve, through established and peaceful channels, the profoundly important issues which motivate this demonstration of your concern."

That same day, after voting to reexamine research policy, the Academic Senate called a special meeting for April 17 (two days after the University Committee on Research Policy was to release its report). The senate unanimously endorsed the statement made by Pitzer at the meeting of the board of trustees two days earlier. The senate also resolved that it shared the moral concern inherent in the president's words: "We spend too much on the military, on means to kill people, and not enough on constructive things to help people." Other resolutions passed at the meeting were that the board of trustees should hold open meetings on the question, that they should report fully to the Stanford community, and that the senate had responsibility for policies controlling research.

Friday, April 11: President Pitzer again asked the protesters to leave AEL, warning that otherwise he "would be obliged to initiate proceedings" through the Judicial Council. Meanwhile, support for the A3M and the sit-in "poured into AEL from campus living and eating units, in addition to 1200 student solidarity statements." A group called Concerned Faculty for SRI voted to support the "pacific" occupation of AEL, on the ground that the demonstrators were acting under "a strongly held moral imperative." It encouraged the protesters to allow persons not engaged in war-connected research to continue work in the laboratory.

Monday, April 14: The University Committee on Research Policy held a two-and-one-half-hour open hearing, attended by two hundred fifty students and faculty members. About one hundred Young Americans for Freedom staged a counterdemonstration outside AEL, protesting "mob rule" and "coercion." The staff at AEL reported that the presence of hundreds of protesters had halted normal work.

President Pitzer declined to release his private letter to the board of trustees requesting changes in the structure of the board. John Gardner, a trustee, was named chairman of a five-person committee to recommend possible changes.

Tuesday, April 15: The University Committee on Research Policy released its report. Nine members recommended that the university sell SRI, servering all ties. Three members—two students and a professor—said SRI should be retained and closely controlled. They felt its sale would destroy the opportunity for the university to establish guidelines that would prevent future undesirable research and channel the SRI resources into more socially responsible activities.

The Academic Senate passed a resolution stating: "The senate desires a significant change in the university research policy, greater than that proposed in the April 15 majority report of the Committee on Research Policy." The senate protested the secrecy surrounding research applications and the failure to publish certain research results.

Thursday, April 17: President Pitzer released a letter to the campus community reporting the position of the administration. In it, he said:

> My resolution has been to manage this situation
> by appeal to the moral commitment, to a free community

of learning. That commitment continues, as it will continue no matter what actions are taken, in the name of morality, which actually threaten the very existence of the university.

After twice notifying those occupying AEL that their acts violated the Campus Disruption Policy—a policy ratified by representative faculty and student bodies—an earnest effort was made to allow those committing what seemed to be an act of conscientious civil disobedience to identify themselves. Authorized faculty and staff persons asked students to give their names as violating campus policies in the interest of a higher cause.

Instead of complying with established procedures and obligations, almost all persons confronted defied the interviewers. One interviewer, a respected member of the faculty, was told that if he returned to the scene of the demonstration he would be bodily attacked.

Pitzer praised the demonstrators for their decision not to damage property or to tamper with classified files and pointed out that the university had an obligation to the federal government to observe that commitment. He called the demonstration "an ugly, sometimes fierce threat to and infringement upon the rights of researchers to research, students to study, and teachers to teach." The importance of the issue was not in question, he added. "I believe the national priorities must be adjusted to the general welfare, and research on means of destruction must yield to research on the instrument of peace."

One A3M member wrote a letter to the *Stanford Daily* objecting to some of Pitzer's remarks. He said students would not give their names to interviewers because they had signed a solidarity statement. "This decision was arrived at to avoid having only a minority of protesters identified, as undoubtedly would occur through haphazard name-taking." He questioned Pitzer's implication that demonstrators were "ill-mannered ruffians," adding that "a few tired demonstrators, fearful or frustrated, may have at times made foolish threats to those whose presence seemed to threaten them."

Most students, however, seemed to approve of Pitzer's

handling of the situation. An editorial in the *Stanford Daily* of April 15 praised him for showing "great restraint and intelligence" and for seeing "beyond the sit-in to the issues."

The Stanford Judicial Council, after ten hours of deliberation on Thursday, decided that the sit-in at the AEL "constituted a disruption of an approved activity of the university" and that President Pitzer was justified, under the Legislative and Judicial Act, in using emergency powers to end the sit-in. It suggested that he declare the AEL and surrounding area closed to all persons for one week and that any student remaining there face suspension. It also expressed the fear that, if the sit-in continued, federal troops might be sent to the campus. The vote was five to two, the dissenting members being students. They argued that, even if extraordinary circumstances existed, it was not consistent with the charter for the SJC to recommend that the president impose sanctions on individual students without a hearing. "An important reason for the promulgation of the charter last spring was to protect students in political cases such as this one."

Friday, April 18: A mass meeting of about six hundred students decided to end the nine-day sit-in at AEL but to resume it if the protesters did not get satisfaction within the week. Tensions had mounted, and demonstrators feared that federal forces would enter the campus if they continued to occupy AEL.

Seven hundred members of the Academic Council met and gave President Pitzer a standing ovation for his "restraint and firmness" in handling the demonstration. They also empowered him to close AEL for a week, joined him in his commitment to the principle that "Stanford shall live by procedures of due process," and pledged themselves to continued dialogue with the rest of the university community in seeking solutions to the problems encountered.

Student body President Denis Hayes called an unprecedented meeting in Frost Amphitheater, attended by about eight thousand students, faculty members, and concerned citizens of the Stanford community. A variety of speakers (including A3M members and SRI staff) talked about the demonstration and about war-related research. Professor Wolfgang Panofsky, director of the Stanford Linear Accelerator Center, said that a university "should exercise

collective moral restraint as to what kind of work it advances."
Joshua Lederberg, Nobel laureate and executive head of the department of genetics, told the audience: "The real problem is not the laboratory work here but the disease of militarism and nationalism and its effect on society. I can't blame you for reacting to changes in the last few years. However, if the use of bodies instead of brains is the best you can think of, God help us all."

In a poll, 3073 of the students voting felt that the sit-in had attracted attention to the problem, while 203 felt that it had not. A slim majority indicated that they would participate in "a sit-in or some similar means of protest" if the board of trustees did not "positively respond to the desire of the Stanford community regarding research at Stanford and SRI" or if it did not resolve "the future relationship between the two institutions by May 14."

The A3M proposed a number of resolutions to the student body for approval: that war-related research be ended; that a Center for Action Toward Research for Peaceful Purposes be established; that a campuswide analysis of research for a peaceful society be conducted the following Monday, with speeches, rallies, and seminars; and that the board of trustees be pressured to come to an early decision about war-related research.

Tuesday, April 22: At the opening session of the Day of Concern, faculty members and protest leaders commended students for their behavior during the sit-in and for the position of "real power" in which they had ended it. Various faculty members took different positions on the subject of classified research. For instance, Leonard Schiff, chairman of the Academic Senate, said that "free exchange of information is vital." Dean Pettit of the engineering school asked: "How much is going to be sacrificed at Stanford as the war drags on and decision-makers do not respond to the indirect forcing of their hands?" William Baxter, chairman of the University Committee on Research Policy, said that the individual researcher has "the right to refuse" to work on a project that is personally repugnant to him, but it is "absolutely immoral to have a collective judgment made that he can't pursue research."

Thursday, April 24: The Academic Senate declared that "the principle of openness in research—the principle of access by all interested persons to the underlying data, to the processes, and to the final results of research—is of overriding importance." It approved a set of guidelines that would permit one or more researchers access to classified information when their projects would be "significantly advanced" by this knowledge. The guidelines also provided that final results would not be restricted with respect to publication and that persons without security clearance should still have access to significant portions of a project.

In an address to the Academic Senate, Dean Pettit said that plans had been made for an "orderly phasing out of several classified contracts" at AEL. The decision had been made, he said, because of the "evident loss of faculty support necessary for the pursuit of this activity in a university." He also remarked that he and William Rambo, head of AEL, had been subjected to "specific, very intense pressure" and that the only way a professor could escape such an inquisition would be to work on only those projects that have no possible application.

Tuesday, April 29: The Academic Senate met in closed session for more than five hours as a committee of the whole. At about the same time, A3M members were discussing tactics at Tressider Memorial Union. No immediate decisions were reached.

The Coalition for an Academic Community (CAC), a newly formed group that opposed the tactics of A3M, distributed two thousand handbills warning that "any community in which the citizens do not protect individuals from coercion from self-appointed groups—minority and majority—cannot remain free."

Wednesday, April 30, 2 P.M.: A five-man committee of the board of trustees held hearings that were broadcast over the campus radio station and on closed-circuit television to Memorial Auditorium. The committee heard five SRI members, five faculty members (selected by the Steering Committee of the Academic Council), and twelve students (chosen by the Associated Students Committee on Nominations). Although petitions demanding an open meeting of the entire board, rather than a committee hearing, had been signed by thirty-five hundred people and turned over to the board, the committee hearings were held to learn what various people felt about the Stanford-SRI problem rather than to indicate the opinions or intentions of the trustees.

One SDS member commented later that the involvement of

Stanford in war-related research was "enraging to thousands of people," and felt it both "very sad" and "arrogant" that the board did not act on their concerns. She told Trustee John Gardner: "You're talking about preserving the right of researchers to do research and we're asking you if you believe that the people of the world have a right to live. . . . We're asking you if researchers have the right to do research which helps murder people."

Wednesday, April 30, 4:30 P.M.: Doron Weinberg, a law school teaching fellow and A3M spokesman, led a walkout and called a movement meeting. From 5:00 to 6:45 P.M., seven hundred A3M supporters debated their course of action and then adjourned for the evening. Later that night, about eight hundred students jammed into Tressider to hear Black Student Union speaker Don Edwards urge another sit-in. The first confused vote showed that the majority supported this idea. To clarify the voting, the house was then divided by having persons walk to different sides of the room. The meeting chairman announced that the vote was 450 in favor of the sit-in and 280 against. At this point the group, which had swelled to nine hundred, moved to Dinkelspiel to choose a target for the demonstration.

Thursday, May 1: After a brief scuffle with YAF members, the A3M supporters broke in the glass doors and entered Encina Hall, nerve center of the administration. Shortly afterward, Dean of Students Joel Smith arrived and ordered them to leave. They refused to comply and summoned a general meeting on the second floor. Meanwhile, President Pitzer was taking steps to get an injunction. He also authorized Provost Lyman to summon the Santa Clara county sheriff to deal with the demonstrators. The next day he explained to the Academic Senate:

> The five available members of the Faculty Consultative Group on Campus Disorders unanimously recommended this action. We were all reluctant to reach this decision, but the willful entrance into files of great importance to the university . . . left no reasonable choice. Among the documents stolen were detailed budgets, including individual salary information for most of the university. Preliminary arrangements had been made

with the sheriff's associates in order to handle such a situation without violence and with reasonable opportunity for anyone to avoid arrest. . . . Today we have implemented the temporary suspensions of those identified last night as remaining in Encina after the building was declared closed. . . .

We are also in the process of seeking an injunction or restraining order from the appropriate legal authorities to bring restraint against both outsiders and those now suspended if they persist in destructive acts or in violation of the terms of their suspension.

At 2:30 A.M., Dean Smith returned to the building with about twenty faculty members and told the demonstrators that they would be suspended if they did not leave within fifteen minutes. At 7:30 A.M., more than 125 law enforcement officers arrived on campus accompanied by volunteer faculty observers, in accord with arrangements established in advance to help protect the rights of students. The students left the building as ordered. There were no arrests. Estimated damage to the building was more than one thousand dollars. No files were damaged, though they had been opened and examined.

Monday, May 5: The A3M supporters staged a mass meeting in the old union courtyard. The number of students temporarily barred from attending classes because of their participation in the Encina Hall occupation rose to sixty.

Monday, May 12: About eight hundred students participated in a "political carnival" to protest war-related research. The A3M sponsored a boycott of classes. It estimated that attendance in large humanities and social science classes was down to about 40 percent of normal, and classes in the sciences were down to about 70 percent. In classes having midterms, attendance was about 100 percent.

Tuesday, May 13: The board of trustees, meeting in San Francisco, decided to sever formal ties between SRI and Stanford. The university's top four elected student leaders said that the board, "as it is presently constituted, signs its own death warrant. . . . We feel that no action that the students might take within the university can change that decision. . . . The question then becomes how can the objectionable research at sri be halted. We must now focus the community's attention on sri and its activities."

Charles Anderson, sri president, called the board's decision "sound and appropriate." In addition, sri adopted a policy not to engage in research projects dealing directly with the development of weapons of chemical and biological warfare.

Wednesday, May 14–Thursday, May 15: Members of the a3m marched by candlelight to the sri Hanover Street facility after voting to disrupt work at the building. The protest ended when one hundred fifty policemen used tear gas to disperse the crowd. Sixteen people were arrested.

Tuesday, May 19: Administrators of sri obtained a temporary restraining order enjoining twenty-seven individuals and twelve organizations from "repeated trespass and unlawful interference with lawful business." Affadavits were signed by President Anderson of sri, other sri employees, several yaf members, and the Stanford Community of the Right. The organizations enjoined included the a3m, sds, the Stanford United Christian Ministry staff, the Peninsula Red Guard, the Committee for New Politics of the United Student Movement, the Palo Alto Concerned Citizens, the Mid-Peninsula Free University, the North Santa Clara Peace and Freedom Party, and American Federation of Teachers Local 1816.

Tuesday, May 27: The United States Permanent Subcommittee on Investigations subpoenaed Stanford University records on twelve organizations and ninety individuals. The records were to be handed over by June 3. (About half the organizations had no connection with Stanford.)

Goals and Changes. The protesters had wanted to arouse the Stanford community to protest against war-related research undertaken by Stanford University personnel, specifically sri. They also sought to influence the administration and the board of trustees to take action that would bring sri under closer university control and would thus lead to a cessation of war-related research. A third goal was to inform the Stanford community about the unresponsiveness of the board of trustees and to question the characteristics and functions desirable for a university trustee. This examination was intended to bring about changes in the composition of the board.

The spring 1969 protest had several outcomes, some favorable to the A3M and some not. On the issues connected with SRI, the board of trustees requested on April 18 that a moratorium be imposed on war-related research contracts until it had studied the situation and reached a decision. Then, on May 13, the board announced that Stanford was selling SRI. This outcome was not a victory for A3M, since it meant that SRI was no longer under effective university control. However, SRI announced that, on the recommendation of its Policy Committee, it would not engage in research activities that related directly to the development of chemical and biological warfare weapons.

On April 24, the Academic Senate announced new guidelines for research policies. Members of A3M called these "a token meaningless concession," however. The Stanford community grew increasingly aware of some of the issues and problems surrounding research at the university. Administrators, faculty members, students, and citizens of the community all made statements of concern.

Ill feeling was engendered within the university community, particularly over the events at Encina Hall of May 1. According to an account in the *Stanford Daily* of May 23, the A3M had moved "toward increased militancy and therefore diminished support." A number of students were suspended and could not attend classes. The protest came to the attention of the Senate Permanent Subcommittee on Investigations (the McClellan Committee), which subpoenaed the records of organizations and individuals.

There was some possibility that the structure, composition, and function of the Board of Trustees would be changed to some extent, depending on the recommendations of the committee appointed by President Pitzer.

VI

OUTCOMES

The impact of protests on the institutions and individuals experiencing them is perhaps the aspect of campus unrest that has been least studied, even though it may, in the final analysis, be the most important legacy of the student movement (see Chapter Three). In this chapter, we assess some of the consequences of protests, particularly the question: What changes do protests bring about in the institution, in administrators, and in students (both those who participate and those who merely observe)?

The data are drawn from three principal sources: periodic surveys of institutions to learn about protest; files of longitudinal data on students; and interviews conducted with administrators at the case study institutions. The first two sources have the advantage of reflecting changes in institutions and students because they contain repeated measures of the same variables at several points in time. Our basic approach was to determine whether particular types of changes were related to the occurrence or nonoccurrence of the several categories of protests.

Impact on Institutions

Chapter Four summarized the results of a detailed analysis of 103 protests that occurred in the 1969–1970 academic year. Among the outcomes discussed were the immediate impact of protest on the day-to-day life of the campus and its long-range impact, as measured by institutional changes. In particular, we examined the issues, participants, and events associated with impact in an effort to learn the antecedent conditions and the nontemporal factors related to change. This chapter takes a somewhat broader view, examining the relationship between campus unrest and change over a longer time span and seeking findings that can be generalized to the national population.

Table 3 lists specific institutional changes that were introduced in 1968–1969 and 1970–1971. Data are from the two national surveys (Bayer and Astin, 1969, 1971). The first two columns of figures indicate the proportion of institutions experiencing severe protest that introduced a specific change. A severe protest was defined as one that involved one or more of the following violent or disruptive acts: burning or bombing a building; breaking into or wrecking a building or its furnishings; destruction of records, files, or papers; conducting marches, rallies, or picket lines accompanied by physical violence, such as fights between demonstrators and counterdemonstrators; occupying a building; obstructing the entrance to a building; detaining officials; blocking traffic or streets; interrupting a school function; staging a general campus strike or boycott of classes; engaging in any other incident that resulted in persons being injured or killed. Examples of incidents not defined as severe are silent vigils, circulation of petitions, and nonviolent campus marches, picketing, or rallies. The last two columns of figures indicate the proportion of the national population of institutions that made a given change, whether they had experienced protest or not.

Two facts emerge clearly. First, a substantial proportion of all institutions implemented significant changes in the two academic years under consideration. Some of the more common changes were curricular revisions and introduction of new programs (including ethnic studies), formation of new committees or study groups, granting greater student representation on existing committees, establishment of special admissions policies for minority group students, liberalization of parietal rules, reforms in the judicial process, alterations in the grading system and in graduation requirements, and hiring more black faculty or administrators. Few changes were

made with respect to war-related issues, such as termination of
ROTC, discontinuation of war-related research, and abolishment of
recruiting on campus. These findings are consistent with those reported in Chapter Four; that is, institutions were much more
responsive to racial and to academic and student life protests than
to war-related protests. The second fact emerging from the table is
that 1970–1971 was marked by fewer major changes in policies,
programs, and facilities than 1968–1969. This difference does not
necessarily mean that administrators were growing more intransigent
or more resistant to change and innovation; it may mean simply that
a given institution had already initiated changes by 1970–1971 and
could go no further.

To what extent can these changes be attributed to the pressure of unrest on campus? A comparison of the first two columns
and the last two columns of figures suggests that protests played a
significant role. In most cases, the proportion of institutions adopting
a particular change was much higher among institutions that had
experienced severe protests than among the total population of
institutions. This was particularly true for the establishment of
ethnic studies programs: more than twice as many disturbed institutions as total institutions introduced such programs in 1968–1969. A
similar difference existed with respect to the establishment of special
admissions policies for minority group students in 1968–1969,
though by 1970–1971 the proportions were about equal for the two
groups of institutions.

While these findings suggest a causal link between campus
protests and institutional changes, an alternative (or perhaps supplementary) explanation is possible. It could be argued that protest-
vulnerable institutions were more likely to institute changes not only
because they experienced more unrest but also because of attributes
that characterize them. As we noted in Chapters Two and Three,
institutions that experienced protest tended to be, among other
things, larger and more selective than institutions that did not
experience protest. It could be that differences such as these, rather
than the occurrence of unrest per se, accounted for their greater
tendency to make changes.

To explore this possibility, we performed certain additional
analyses using data from the 1968–1969 survey of unrest and change

Table 3. INCIDENCE OF CHANGE WITH AND WITHOUT PROTEST

| | Percentage Making Changes[a] | | | |
| | Institutions with Severe Protests | | All Institutions | |
Changes	1968–1969 (N =524)	1970–1971 (N = 462)	1968–1969	1970–1971 (N = 2362)
Ethnic studies courses, programs, or departments instituted	63.3	23.2	28.0	16.9
Women's studies courses or programs instituted		14.5		6.1
Honors program instituted	78.2	1.7	49.5	5.2
Other major curricular changes implemented		35.9		36.3
Special admissions policies established for minority group members	29.8	6.3	13.3	6.0
More black faculty or administrators hired	b	40.0	b	27.4
More women faculty or administrators hired	b	14.5	b	9.1
Procedures for awarding tenure or promotion changed	b	18.4	b	13.5
New procedures instituted for formal evaluation of teacher effectiveness	b	35.5	b	21.0
Parietal rules liberalized	55.1	41.3	31.5	32.5
Grading system changed		26.6		23.8

Judiciary process changed		27.3		22.7
Housing changes (black student housing, coed dormitories)	64.3	19.3	46.2	14.9
Class attendance regulations changed		8.9		12.6
Graduation requirements changed		17.1		18.0
Students allowed more voice or representation on existing committees	71.9	45.5	51.2	40.7
New committees or study groups formed on campus	84.5	48.5	44.7	39.2
ROTC program terminated	1.1	1.5	0.4	0.5
ROTC program altered or made elective	9.5	8.7	2.9	2.7
Some campus research for the military or other classified research discontinued	0.8	0.0	0.2	0.0
Procedures for job recruiting on campus altered	[b]	8.2	[b]	5.0
More minority labor employed by institutions	[b]	13.4	[b]	9.6
Plans for construction or expansion of facilities altered	[b]	22.7	[b]	13.7
Other	[b]	10.2	[b]	3.9

Source: Bayer and Astin, 1971.

[a] Weighted population estimates. Estimated population counts are based on the 1968 ACE national norms stratification design with weights based on the 1970–1971 campus unrest survey respondents. For a detailed description of sampling and weighting procedures, see Creager, 1968.
[b] Data not available.

(see Astin and Bayer, 1971). Because so few changes were made on war-related issues, only two major categories of institutional change were considered: those having to do with racial policies (such as the establishment of black studies programs, the introduction of special admissions policies for minority group members, and the hiring of more black faculty members and administrators) and those having to do with student power (for example, increased student representation on existing committees, student participation in curriculum planning and revision, and other changes giving students a greater role in governance). Not included in the second category were minor changes in institutional policy such as the formation of special study groups or ad hoc committees involving students. Our intention was to examine the independent effects of issues, tactics, and institutional characteristics on changes by means of multiple regression analyses. Such analyses permit us to partial out the effects of all other sets of factors and look only at the effects of the set of factors under consideration. For instance, the impact of protest tactics by themselves can be examined, after controlling for the effects of student input characteristics, protest issues, and institutional characteristics.

The results of these analyses showed clearly that the protest issues were related to the type of change made during a given year. Thus, the occurrence of student power protests made it much more likely that the institution would give students a greater voice in governance; similarly, racial protests were associated with changes in racial policies. In addition, protests over facilities and student life often led to changes in student power (showing a relationship between the two types of academic life issues). Finally, protests that grew out of previously unresolved protests or out of students' objections to the handling of previous protests were associated with changes in racial policy. (Nonresolution of a previous protest was also found to be a common precipitating factor in the racial protests examined in Chapter Four.) Protests over racial policies appeared to be in competition with other kinds of protests; changes on racial policies were unlikely to occur during the same year if there were protests over student life or student power issues.

Looking at the relation between protest tactics and racial policy or student power changes, we find that increases in student power were granted independent of the tactics used. When protesters staged sit-ins (a disruptive tactic that was found in the newspaper study to be common in protests over racial policies), changes in racial policies were not likely to be made. Violence was unrelated to such changes. Disruptive tactics other than sit-ins, however, did tend to be associated with some change by the institution in its racial policies. In short, institutions seemed somewhat more willing to make concessions to black students when their tactics were extreme but not violent.

No institutional characteristic was related to changes in student power, a finding that suggests that different types of institutions were making such changes at about the same rate and in proportion to the amount of protest activity they experienced. There were, however, some significant relationships between institutional characteristics and changes in racial policies. Universities seemed to be changing their racial policies at a slower rate than colleges, especially in light of the type and frequency of protest at these institutions. To a lesser degree, large institutions and art schools lagged in changing their racial policies. In contrast, four-year colleges were more inclined to make such changes than other institutions.

These findings confirm some of the protest patterns described in Chapter Four. Protests over racial and student power issues usually resulted in fairly immediate institutional change (see Figures 1 and 2). But what of the longer range picture? The analyses so far have been limited to protests and changes that occurred during a single academic year. But there are almost certainly many institutions that delayed making changes until a year following the protest that pushed for the change. To get a better fix on the situation, we collated the data from several surveys covering the period between 1966 and 1971. There were 111 institutions for which we had complete data on two types of institutional changes—the introduction of ethnic studies courses, programs, or departments, and the establishment of special admissions policies for minority-group members—and on related protest occurrences; for 109 institutions we had complete data on increases in student representation on policy committees and related protests. We set out to answer two basic questions: Are these three specific kinds of changes influenced by prior unrest? Do these changes forestall further unrest over the same or similar issues?

The findings from this analysis (Table 4) have certain limitations, since our information on the sequence of protest and change before the 1969–1970 academic year was incomplete. Moreover, when protests and related changes occurred during the same academic year—as was frequently the case—we could not always be sure that the protest preceded the change. Two other points should be made about these data: many institutions had multiple protests on the same issue; and the institutions that made changes during 1969–1971 may also have made related changes during an earlier period.

By the end of the 1970–1971 academic year, almost all the institutions in the sample had provided for greater student representation on policy committees and had introduced special admissions policies for minority group members. One-fifth of the sample, however, had not established ethnic studies programs by that time. Institutions were particularly quick to respond to demands for special admissions policies; almost three-fourths had introduced such policies before 1969–1970. Moreover, 14 percent of the institutions made this change even when they were not under pressure from protests about it. In contrast, fewer than one-fourth of the institutions had made concessions with respect to student power before 1969–1970. Most of those that introduced such changes did so after 1969.

Several protest patterns emerged. During the most recent years, protests tended to occur either before a related change or before and during the year of the change; there were few cases in which protests occurred only in the same year that the change was made. The explanation is simply that most of the institutions had protests relating to these issues before 1969–1970. Coming rather late in the protest era, these changes apparently forestalled further protests on the same or similar issues. But this did not hold true for earlier years, when further protests on similar issues occurred even after a change had been made, particularly in the case of special admissions policies for minority group members, a change that by no means precluded subsequent unrest over racial policies. It seems

Table 4. SEQUENCE OF THREE TYPES OF INSTITUTIONAL CHANGES AND PROTESTS ON RELATED ISSUES

Protest and Change	Student Representation on Policy Committees (N = 109)	Ethnic Studies Courses, Programs, or Departments (N = 111)	Special Admissions Policies for Minority-Group Members (N = 111)
Change (feature introduced) prior to 1969–1970 only	23.9	17.1	73.9
Related protest 1966–1969 only	9.2	9.0	27.0
Related protest 1966–1969 and after	11.9	7.2	25.2
Related protest after 1966–1969 only	0.0	0.0	7.2
No related protest	2.8	0.9	14.4
Change (feature introduced) in 1969–1970 or in 1970–1971	74.3	62.2	20.7
Related protest before change only	36.7	19.8	5.4
Related protest before and same year as change	21.1	21.6	9.0
Related protest before (and/or same year) and after change	6.4	9.0	4.5
Related protest same year as change only	0.9	2.7	1.8
Related protest after change only	0.0	2.7	0.0
No related protest	9.2	6.3	0.0
No change (feature not introduced)	1.8	20.7	5.4
Had related protest	0.9	11.7	3.6
No related protest	0.9	9.0	1.8

that, even though some of the issues were settled, students often sought additional concessions.

In general, in both periods, 1966–1969 and 1969–1971, if a change was introduced without a preceding protest, no related protest was likely to occur. In a few instances, this absence of unrest may be attributable to characteristics of the institution that rendered it relatively unsusceptible to protest; but this cannot be the entire explanation, since most of these institutions had protests about other issues. Perhaps we can interpret the finding to mean that, when an institution introduces a change without the pressure of protest, it in effect preempts students' demands without giving them a sense of victory that might lead them to press for further concessions.

The final point made clear by these data is that, while a specific change was very often preceded by protest on a related issue, protest did not inevitably lead to change. Over half the institutions not introducing a particular change *did* experience a related protest.

To summarize, the analyses indicated that protests tended to "work." Protests on either racial policies or student power issues were more often than not followed by substantive institutional changes. Since these relationships held even after student input and institutional characteristics were taken into account, the link would seem to be a direct causal one: protest leads to change.

Many institutions implemented changes without the pressure of protest, however. In other words, protest was not a necessary condition of change on some campuses; indeed, changes undertaken in the absence of protest apparently reduced the chances that a subsequent protest on a related issue would occur. It is possible, of course, that institutions made certain changes with the specific intention of preventing demonstrations. In this sense, then, it is arguable that the national climate of unrest—created by its prevalence on other campuses—can be an important determinant of institutional change on campuses where no unrest occurs.

Impact on Administrators

In Chapter Three we summarized data from personal interviews with 101 administrators about their role in campus protests. These interviews included a number of open-ended questions designed to assess how administrators had been affected by unrest. While this information is largely anecdotal, it does provide the subjective responses of a diverse group of administrators.

Generally, administrators agreed that protests resulted in positive changes, the two most important areas being governance of the institution and curricular reform and innovation. Nonetheless, their perceptions of the effect of protest had a bleaker side. Most felt that unrest and student dissatisfaction had resulted in a lessening of their authority. They also complained that more demands were being made on their time; they were overworked and harassed by constant requests to mediate and to undertake public relations tasks. They saw themselves as having frequent and extensive contacts with students; 31 percent claimed that they spent at least eighteen hours a week with students outside the classroom. In short, though many administrators viewed campus unrest as a positive vehicle for change in academic life, they also felt that it had an adverse effect on their own lives. It should be remembered that these administrators were interviewed in spring 1969, when campuses were almost battlegrounds. Some administrators had been subjected to ridicule and verbal attack and had even been locked in buildings by protesters. Little wonder that they were agitated and weary when our interviewers queried them about the protests on their campuses. The following are sample comments from the interviews:

> There have been a number of curriculum changes all over the country. Administrators are far more alert to campus problems. Colleges are becoming more flexible. Many faculty members have become better aware of their broad, overall intellectual responsibilities.

> [One result of protest is that there is now] more student determination in the governance of the institution, academic and nonacademic. [They have] more voice if not vote. The public in general and students are more concerned about national issues.

> I think that university administrators can no longer be, as they once were, simple caretakers of people, keeping things going as they are. [They must be] much more alert

to what people are thinking, what people will want in
the future. You have to be much more willing to work
hard to foresee what sorts of demands are going to be
made of the college so that you can meet those demands
prior to a blowup of some kind.

There's a growing tendency among students and faculty
alike *not* to respect the work of administrators. These
people believe they have the right to determine academic
policies, but they are not responsible for the consequences.
This they push onto the administrators.

[There has been a] change from an authoritative to less
authoritative administration. Now [administrators] think
twice about decisions and are open to student opinions
(from want or necessity).

In general it is true [that administrators have become]
mediators between students and faculty, and that's a
shift from the former position as against faculty and students. I begin to see faculty as conservative and administrators as more innovative.

[Administrators are] the enemy. I can't even say good
morning to a kid without him thinking I'm brewing up
some kind of trouble for him. They hate us.

Impact on Student Participants

The next question to consider is: How does participation in
a campus protest affect the behavior and attitudes of students? The
sample used in examining this question was a group of 5351 students
who entered 178 nationally representative institutions as freshmen in
the fall of 1967 (at which time they completed the Student Information Form) and were followed up in the late summer of 1968,
when they had presumably completed one year of college. There was
an overlap of twenty-seven behavioral items and fifteen attitudinal
items on the two questionnaires (the 1967 SIF and the 1968 follow-
up), thus permitting us to compare students' responses at two points

in time and note changes that had occurred after a one-year exposure to college. In addition, the follow-up questionnaire asked the students to indicate whether they had participated in organized demonstrations during the freshman year.

To isolate the effects of protest participation on the student, it was necessary first to take into account changes in behavior and attitudes that occurred for all students, whether they had engaged in demonstrations or not. As many studies have indicated, certain changes are typical of students during the first year of college. Some of these may be attributable to the maturation process, others to the impact of the general college environment. To assess accurately how students are affected by taking part in a protest, we first had to control for those changes that occur independent of protest participation. This control was accomplished by means of a series of two-stage multiple regression analyses, carried out separately for each of the twenty-seven behavioral outcomes and fifteen attitudinal outcomes under consideration. In the first stage, all student input variables from the SIF were entered into regression until no additional input variable was capable of producing a significant (p less than .05) reduction in the residual sum of squares. The input variables included demographic characteristics such as sex, age, and race; socioeconomic characteristics such as parental income and education; high school grades; degree aspirations; religious background and preference; probable college major; and freshman responses to the behavioral and attitudinal items (the "pretests"). From this first stage, then, we were able to identify the freshman variables that predicted certain changes in behaviors and attitudes. In the second stage of the analysis, after the effects of the freshman input variables were controlled, it was possible to get some idea of the independent effects of protest participation on the attitudes and behaviors of participants. Such statistical controls do not, of course, guarantee that the resulting relationships (presented as partial correlations) reflect causal relationships. One difficulty is that we cannot be certain that the behavior or attitude under consideration actually followed a student's involvement in protest; it may have preceded it. Such ambiguity is inevitable when protest participation cannot be specified precisely in time. While such controls reduce the chances that causal inferences from such partial correlations will be invalid, the investigator is still forced to rely on what seems to be the most plausible explanation with respect to causal relations.

Behavioral Changes in Freshman Year. Both the SIF and the follow-up asked respondents to indicate whether they had engaged in a particular activity frequently (scored 3), occasionally (scored 2), or not at all (scored 1). Table 5 lists the twenty-seven behavior outcomes studied. The first two columns of figures indicate changes that occurred during the freshman year; a positive sign means that the sample students tended to report engaging in the particular behavior more frequently at the end of the freshman year than when they started college; a negative sign indicates that they reported engaging in the behavior less frequently (or not at all) at the end of the freshman year. An increase in the standard deviation means that the students moved further apart on their responses, a decrease indicates that they became more alike in their responses. No overall trend toward either greater homogeneity or greater heterogeneity emerged over the one-year interval; the standard deviations for about half the items increased, whereas the remainder either decreased or remained the same.

Looking at the items related to academic behavior, we find that students were less likely to fail to complete a homework assignment on time in college than they had been in high school, more likely to type their homework assignments, and more likely to study with other students. Such a pattern of changes in work habits may represent a response to the more stringent demands of college. In addition, students became much less likely to miss school because of illness, a change that could be attributable not only to a greater feeling of responsibility in college but also to the likelihood that the student was no longer living at home with parents who might be inclined to keep a child from going to school if he or she was ill. The finding that students grew more inclined to smoke cigarettes and drink beer and less inclined to take vitamins may also reflect this new freedom from parental supervision.

Students also were more likely to oversleep and miss classes or appointments and to sleep or doze in class during their first year of college than they had been in high school. Again, these changes may indicate that an increase in personal freedom led to irregular sleeping habits; another explanation is that the academic pressures

Table 5. Changes in Student Behavior in Freshman Year

Behavioral Item	Changes Between SIF and Follow-up		Correlation between SIF and Follow-up Responses	Stepwise Regression	
	Mean	Standard Deviation		Number of Variables	R
Overslept and missed a class or appointment	+.40ª	+.18ª	.240	19	.41
Drank beer	+.27ª	+.05ª	.556	15	.59
Smoked cigarettes	+.19ª	+.09ª	.710	7	.72
Typed a homework assignment	+.14ª	+.01ª	.412	15	.47
Studied with other students	+.12ª	.00	.280	13	.32
Discussed politics	+.12ª	−.01ª	.462	17	.52
Slept or dozed in class	+.05ª	+.01ª	.447	11	.46
Played bridge	+.05ª	+.08ª	.458	13	.49
Saw a foreign movie	+.03ª	+.01ª	.336	20	.44
Took sleeping pills	+.01	+.03ª	.335	11	.36
Tutored another student	.00	−.04ª	.311	19	.36
Took a tranquilizing pill	.00	+.01ª	.372	12	.40
Played tennis	−.03ª	−.01ª	.415	10	.43
Got a traffic ticket	−.04ª	−.05ª	.250	13	.35
Discussed religion	−.05ª	.00	.393	16	.45
Argued with a teacher in class	−.10ª	−.04ª	.435	22	.51
Was a guest in a teacher's home	−.14ª	−.10ª	.182	18	.35
Asked a teacher for advice after class	−.14ª	−.03ª	.310	16	.36
Failed to complete a homework assignment on time	−.16ª	+.04ª	.342	18	.39
Did extra (unassigned) reading for a course	−.17ª	.00	.353	17	.40
Discussed sports	−.17ª	+.03ª	.612	17	.65
Took vitamins	−.19ª	+.01ª	.502	8	.51
Visited an art gallery or museum	−.19ª	+.03ª	.333	22	.42
Rode on a motorcycle	−.19ª	+.06ª	.449	18	.35
Played chess	−.21ª	−.12ª	.502	13	.55
Took a trip of more than five hundred miles	−.23ª	+.02ª	.261	13	.32
Missed school because of illness	−.29ª	+.06ª	.260	12	.35

ª Significant at $p = .05$.

of the freshman year prevented students from getting sufficient sleep.

Although the tendencies to type homework assignments and to get them in on time may be regarded as desirable changes, others are somewhat discouraging, suggesting a decrease in cultural and intellectual interests. Students visited art galleries and museums much less frequently (though they were slightly more inclined to go to foreign films) and played chess less frequently. In addition, they became less inclined to do unassigned reading for a course, to argue with a teacher in class, or to ask a teacher for advice outside of class. In short, their intellectual vigor and interest in learning seemed to dwindle; they were more interested in simply getting by. Since college is supposed to stimulate independent thought and discussion, these changes are disturbing. The institution—not the student—may be to blame for some of these changes. The lack of interaction between faculty members and students is confirmed by a decrease in the frequency with which students were guests in a teacher's home. The implication is that most colleges are much more impersonal than most high schools. Large lecture classes (typical of the freshman year) and the teachers' lack of interest in teaching (compared to research) may discourage students from seeking out their professors and may also have a depressing effect on their intellectual interests.

Behaviors relating to sports (playing tennis, riding a motorcycle, discussing sports) became less frequent during the college years, whereas certain traditional "collegiate" behaviors (playing bridge, discussing politics, drinking beer, and smoking cigarettes) became more frequent. On the other hand, somewhat inexplicably, students became less inclined to discuss religion or to get traffic tickets. (The latter finding may mean simply that cars were less available to them than when they were living with their parents.) Understandably, students were less apt to take trips of over five hundred miles.

It should be emphasized that we have been looking at behavioral changes during the freshman year. Thus, we cannot tell from these data whether such behaviors as the apparent decline in intellectual and cultural interests and the irregularity of sleeping habits typically persist throughout the four years of college or whether students tend to settle down more and become better adjusted to pressure during the remainder of their college careers.

The third column of figures in Table 5, showing the correlations between responses to the SIF and to the follow-up questionnaire, and the final column, showing the final multiple correlation coefficients from the regression analyses, suggest that the accuracy with which freshman-year behavior can be predicted from behavior during high school varied substantially from item to item. The most predictable behaviors were smoking cigarettes and discussing sports; the least predictable were being a guest in a teacher's home, oversleeping and missing classes, studying with other students, taking long trips, getting traffic tickets, and missing school because of illness. It seems likely that these unpredictable behaviors are highly dependent on the type of college attended (particularly its enrollment size and whether it is a residential or a commuter college).

Behavioral Changes Related to Protest Participation. Having examined behavioral changes typical of all students during the freshman year, we turn now to the results of the second stage of the regression analysis, presented in Table 6. The first column of figures shows the zero-order correlations (that is, before control for student input variables) between protest participation and specific behaviors. The second column shows the partial correlations (that is, the relationship between protest participation and specific behaviors after student input variables have been taken into account). Both the zero-order correlations and the partial correlations of seventeen of the twenty-seven behavioral items were significant, and all were in a positive direction. (Six of the ten remaining behavioral items had significant zero-order correlations, but these shrank to nonsignificance when student input variables were controlled.) This means that student protesters as a group engaged in the listed behaviors more frequently than would be expected on the basis of their freshman input characteristics. All students as a group engaged less frequently in most behaviors during the first year of college than they had in high school (see Table 5). Apparently, protest participation had a "cushioning" effect on the general impact of the college environment. What is more important, the fact that all partial correlations were positive suggests that protest participation is related to an overall increase in activity level.

The behavior most closely associated with participating in protest was discussing politics. This is not surprising, since the very

Table 6. RELATIONS BETWEEN PARTICIPATION
AND BEHAVIORAL CHANGE

Behavioral Item	Zero-order Correlation	Partial Correlation[a]
Discussed politics	.232	.126
Saw a foreign movie	.212	.117
Argued with a teacher in class	.206	.110
Smoked cigarettes	.165	.090
Discussed religion	.147	.086
Did extra (unassigned) reading for a course	.156	.080
Overslept and missed a class or appointment	.144	.059
Took a tranquilizing pill	.093	.059
Visited an art gallery or museum	.154	.058
Was a guest in a teacher's home	.110	.053
Asked a teacher for advice after class	.092	.051
Drank beer	.119	.050
Rode on a motorcycle	.068	.043
Typed a homework assignment	.082	.042
Took a trip of more than five hundred miles	.083	.040
Tutored another student	.088	.033
Missed school because of illness	.060	.027

[a] After control for student input variables. A correlation of .027 is significant at $p = .05$.

act of becoming involved in a protest probably stimulates the student's interest in political matters, either during the demonstration itself or as part of the postmortem.

Unlike the typical student, the protester tended to maintain an interest in intellectual and cultural matters and to develop closer ties with instructors, as indicated by the behaviors of arguing with a teacher in class, doing unassigned reading for a course, visiting an art gallery or museum, being a guest in a teacher's home, asking a teacher for advice after class, and tutoring other students.

The finding that participation in a demonstration was positively related to discussing religion deserves comment. One possible interpretation is that protests at church-affiliated institutions may often have concerned regulations such as mandatory attendance at chapel or other manifestations of religious control of the college. Since protesters were more likely than nonprotesters to say that they had no religious preference (see Chapter Three), they might have come into conflict with the more orthodox religious influences on campus and thus have been more apt to argue about religious matters.

In light of the stereotype of the student radical as one who eschews alcohol, it is somewhat surprising to find that participation in protest was associated with more frequently drinking beer, smoking cigarettes, and taking tranquilizing pills. One must keep in mind, however, that we are here discussing protest participants, not the much smaller group of protest leaders, who were often of the radical left. The most likely explanation of these relationships is that participation in protest made the student more open to other experiences.

As was pointed out previously, the causal relation between protest participation and the behaviors being considered is confused by our lack of information on which preceded the other. Despite this uncertainty, one thing seems clear from these analyses: participation in protest during the freshman year was associated with a generally increased level of activity in academic, interpersonal, and other areas. Compared with their nonparticipant classmates, protesters interacted more with their professors and fellow students, were more inclined to go to art galleries, museums, and foreign films, and had a greater predilection for traveling and for using alcohol and cigarettes. This complex of behaviors also suggests that protesters were more susceptible to stress and tension. That the stress may have had physical effects is suggested by the increased tendency of protesters to take tranquilizers and to miss school because of illness.

Attitudinal Changes in Freshman Year. Both the 1967 SIF and the summer 1968 follow-up questionnaire included a number of items that tapped the students' attitudes on various controversial questions relating to campus life and to the "outside" world. Respondents were asked to indicate whether they agreed strongly (scored 4), agreed somewhat (scored 3), disagreed somewhat (scored 2), or disagreed strongly (scored 1) with each of the statements. Table 7 shows changes in the mean scores and the standard deviations for fifteen attitudinal items common to both questionnaires.

Table 7. CHANGES IN STUDENT ATTITUDES IN FRESHMAN YEAR

Attitudinal Item	Changes between SIF and Follow-up		Correlation between SIF and Follow-up Responses	Stepwise Regression	
	Mean	Standard Deviation		Number of Variables	R
The voting age should be lowered to eighteen	+.32[a]	−.06[a]	.492	12	.52
Faculty promotions should be based in part on student evaluations	+.26[a]	+.02[a]	.335	18	.38
Realistically, an individual person can do little to bring about changes in our society	+.11	+.06[a]	.304	15	.35
Scientists should publish their findings regardless of the possible consequences	+.09[a]	+.02[a]	.355	9	.37
Parents should be discouraged from having large families	+.08[a]	+.03[a]	.532	13	.56
Colleges would be improved if organized sports were deemphasized	+.02[a]	+.07[a]	.440	23	.51
Women should be subject to the draft	+.01[a]	+.03[a]	.522	8	.53

Students from disadvantaged social backgrounds should be given preferential treatment in college admissions	.00	+.04[a]	.335	14	.40
Most college officials have been too lax in dealing with student protests on campus	−.02[a]	+.08[a]	.404	22	.49
My beliefs and attitudes are similar to those of most other college students	−.08[a]	+.04[a]	.374	18	.43
The chief benefit of a college education is that it increases one's earning power	−.22[a]	.00	.447	25	.53
College officials have the right to ban persons with extreme views from speaking on campus	−.25[a]	−.04[a]	.404	22	.49
The activities of married women are best confined to the home and family	−.29[a]	.00	.507	18	.57
Student publications should be cleared by college officials	−.30[a]	+.01[a]	.441	19	.52
College faculty are more competent than students to specify curriculum	−.34[a]	+.07[a]	.231	23	.32

[a] Significant at $p = .05$.

The results show the changes in attitude typical of all students, protest participants and nonparticipants alike, during the one-year interval between college entrance and the end of the freshman year.

Almost all the standard deviations increased slightly, indicating that students as a group become more polarized in their opinions during the freshman year. The low correlations (third column of Table 7) between responses to the items on the SIF and to the same items on the follow-up indicate that, apart from the changes in the mean for all students, the attitudes of individual students changed considerably during the freshman year. The low multiple correlations (shown in the last column) indicate that such changes are very difficult to predict from freshman input characteristics.

It should be pointed out that most of these items have rather low reliabilities, estimated to range from .43 to .74 on the basis of a one-week test-retest (Boruch and Creager, 1972). The attitudes of individual students, therefore, were more stable than the correlations in the table would indicate. If the observed correlations are corrected for attenuation due to low reliability, the mean of the corrected correlations is .673, compared to .408 for the uncorrected correlations. These reliability estimates may be somewhat off, both because some real changes in attitude may have occurred over the one-week interval and because the test and retest were necessarily lacking in complete independence. The "true" correlations probably lie somewhere between the corrected and the uncorrected values.)

The students as a group tended to become more liberal in their attitudes during the freshman year of college. One of the most marked changes was the increase in agreement with the statement that the voting age should be lowered to eighteen. (At the time, the voting age had, of course, not yet been lowered by the Twenty-sixth Amendment, which went into effect in July 1971.) Students also became more likely to reject the conventional views that a married woman's activities were best confined to the home and family and that the chief benefit of a college education was an increase in one's earning power. They gave greater support to two other controversial issues: discouraging large families and publishing scientific findings regardless of the consequences.

On matters relating directly to college life, the shift toward liberalism was particularly apparent. After one year of college, students were much less inclined to agree that the faculty were more competent than students to specify the college curriculum, that student publications should be cleared by college officials, and that the administration had the right to ban extremist speakers from the campus; they were much more inclined to agree that faculty promotions should be based in part on student evaluations. It may be that these changes in attitudes reflect growing self-confidence and independence. They also suggest that, after exposure to the college environment, students were apt to grow more skeptical, and even cynical, about the competence of those in authority.

A tendency toward pessimism is reflected in their increased acceptance of the statement that the individual can do little to bring about changes in our society and in their greater inclination to feel that their attitudes and beliefs differed from those of most other college students.

On several items, students shifted only slightly (though the changes were still statistically significant). By the end of the freshman year, they were somewhat more inclined to feel that college would be improved if sports were deemphasized and that women should be subject to the draft; they were somewhat less inclined to feel that college officials had been too lax in dealing with protesters, but the variation on this last item increased considerably over the one-year interval. In other words, more students agreed and disagreed strongly, indicating that, after a year of college, their attitudes had become more polarized on the issue of campus unrest.

Perhaps the only finding inconsistent with the shift toward greater liberalism was the constancy of the belief that students from disadvantaged backgrounds should be given preferential treatment in admissions; there was no change in the mean score of 2.23 over the one-year period.

Attitudinal Changes Related to Protest Participation. The summer 1968 follow-up questionnaire asked about the student's participation, during the freshman year, in three types of protests: against racial discrimination, against a college administrative policy, and against the Vietnam War. (These categories correspond roughly with those used in Chapters Four and Five—racial policies, academic and student life, and war-related or social issues—except that the newspaper study and the documentation study were both limited to protests directed against the institution, whereas the follow-up survey included protests directed at agencies and events outside the institution.) Because the number of attitudinal outcomes analyzed was smaller than the number of behavioral outcomes, we were able to accommodate more predictor variables in our analyses. We thus considered the impact on attitudes not just of protest participation but of participation in specific kinds of protest.

Table 8 presents the results of these analyses, showing the zero-order correlations and the partial correlations for the twelve attitudinal items that entered the regression with significant weights for at least two of the three measures of protest participation. Nine of these had significant partial correlations with participation in all three types of protest. Three items that do not appear in the table are those on discouraging parents from having large families, drafting women, and the inability of the individual to effect social change. The implication is that attitudes on these questions were not clearly associated with any tendency toward a liberal or a conservative point of view. The table does include two additional items—a measure of satisfaction with the overall college experience, and an estimate by the students of the probability that they would return to the same college in the fall.

Participation in any of the three types of protests had similar effects on the students' attitudes toward a given statement; there were no reversals in the signs of the partial correlations. Moreover, the signs were in the same direction as the changes in mean scores (Table 7), except for the item about preferential treatment in admissions for disadvantaged college students, where the mean score did not change in the one-year interval, while participants in protest became more inclined to agree with this statement. Since, as we noted, the general tendency of college students is to grow more liberal in their attitudes during the freshman year, we may conclude that participation in protest intensifies this tendency; this is hardly surprising, since we would not expect protesters to become more conservative.

Participation in protest, then, was clearly related to changes in attitude. The nature of this relationship was the same for all three types of protest, though the strength of the relationship varied with the protest category. Before discussing these differences, we must again point out the difficulties of making causal inferences from this type of analysis. The student's attitudes were first assessed during the freshman orientation period, before any possible participation in a college demonstration; they were then reassessed after one year, and the student was asked about participation in any of the three types of protest. Thus, we have no way of knowing from these data what the students' attitudes were immediately before they entered the picket line or signed the petition. It may be that the change in attitude occurred before the student joined a demonstration and that this change was attributable to other factors in the college environment; thus, a change in attitude may be a cause rather than an effect of participation in protest. Equally, protest participation may be an antecedent of, and a factor contributing to, attitude change. There is no way to be certain. We can, however, note associations between protest participation and attitude change.

There was a very strong—and very understandable—association between participation in any of the three kinds of protest and an inclination to disagree with the statement that college officials have been too lax in dealing with campus unrest. Demonstrators in anti-Vietnam protests were most apt to feel this way. Most of the other relationships reflect differences that common sense would suggest, considering the type of protest involved.

For example, participants in demonstrations against racial discrimination grew much more inclined to feel that students from disadvantaged social backgrounds (a description that implies minority group members, to a considerable extent) should be given preferential treatment in admissions. They also came to feel that their attitudes and beliefs were not like those of other college students, a perception that, in the case of black students, may reflect a growing sense of racial identity. (It is worth noting here that black students are also more likely to drop out if they attend a predominately white rather than a predominately black college. See Astin, 1975.)

Participants in demonstrations against college administrative policies, on the other hand, were more likely than other participants to have firm convictions about such campus issues as free speech and student power and to reject the authority of faculty members and administrators. Thus, we find a strong relationship between such

Table 8. RELATIONS BETWEEN PARTICIPATION AND ATTITUDINAL CHANGE

| | Correlation with Participation in Protest[a] | | | | | |
| Attitudinal Item | On Racial Discrimination | | On College Administrative Policy | | On Vietnam War | |
	Zero-order r	Partial r^a	Zero-order r	Partial r^a	Zero-order r	Partial r^a
Students from disadvantaged social backgrounds should be given preferential treatment in college admissions	.158	.102	.062	b	.136	.080
Colleges would be improved if organized sports were deemphasized	.140	.069	.076	.035	.191	.086
The voting age should be lowered to eighteen	.114	.057	.114	.054	.123	.066
Scientists should publish their findings regardless of the possible consequences	0.71	.046	.066	.045	.094	.056
Faculty promotions should be based in part on student evaluations	.088	.038	.100	.071	.094	.036
My beliefs and attitudes are similar to those of most other college students	−.100	−.037	−.050	b	−.122	−.032

The chief benefit of a college education is that it increases one's earning power	$-.123$	$-.048$	$-.042$	b	$-.156$	$-.047$
The activities of married women are best confined to the home and family	$-.131$	$-.045$	$-.095$	$-.044$	$-.164$	$-.053$
College faculty are more competent than students to specify the curriculum	$-.100$	$-.038$	$-.122$	$-.066$	$-.134$	$-.061$
College officials have the right to ban persons with extreme views from speaking on campus	$-.179$	$-.065$	$-.167$	$-.083$	$-.211$	$-.066$
Student publications should be cleared by college officials	$-.163$	$-.062$	$-.181$	$-.107$	$-.220$	$-.072$
Most college officials have been too lax in dealing with student protests on campus	$-.220$	$-.099$	$-.207$	$-.116$	$-.285$	$-.140$
Satisfaction with college	$-.034$	b	$-.086$	$-.061$	$-.066$	$-.036$
Probability of returning in the fall	b	b	b	b	$-.034$	$-.034$

[a] After control for student input variables. A correlation of .027 is significant at $p = .05$.

[b] Not significant.

participation and a tendency to disagree that college officials should have the right to clear student publications and to ban extremist speakers or that faculty members are more competent than students to make decisions about curriculum; and these participants tended to agree that faculty promotions should be based in part on student evaluations. But toward some issues they were relatively indifferent. For instance, there were no significant relationships between participation in protests over administrative policy and attitudes toward the monetary advantages of a college education or preferential treatment in admissions for disadvantaged students. Moreover, these protesters were not particularly inclined to feel that their beliefs and attitudes differed from those of most other college students. Compared to the other two types of protesters, they had little tendency to feel that the voting age should be lowered to eighteen or that sports should be deemphasized.

Involvement in demonstrations against the Vietnam War was associated with an increased desire for change in areas outside university control, such as lowering the voting age, publishing all scientific findings regardless of the consequences, and a less stereotyped role for married women. Antiwar demonstrators also grew more inclined to feel that sports should be deemphasized—a reflection, perhaps, of their greater interest in political affairs and their rejection of traditional college life—and that disadvantaged students should be given preferential treatment in admissions. Their attitudes were generally closer to those of participants in racial protests than of participants in administrative policy protests. For instance, antiwar and racial protesters were about equally inclined to feel, at the end of the freshman year, that their beliefs and attitudes were unlike those of most college students.

It is not surprising to find that demonstrators against administrative policies were most likely to express dissatisfaction with college, though this dissatisfaction had no effect on the likelihood that they would return to the same college in the fall. There was a slighter relation between demonstrating against the Vietnam War and dissatisfaction with college, but in this case, the students often indicated that there was little likelihood that they would return to the same college in the fall. The partial correlations between participation in demonstrations against racial discrimination and both satisfaction with college and probability of returning to the same college were nonsignificant, which may indicate that such protests were directed at discrimination outside the institution.

Summary. The analyses of the impact of protest participation on students' behavior and attitudes during the freshman year give a mixed picture. Participation seemed to retard general college effects on certain behaviors and to accentuate general college effects on attitudes. Involvement in demonstrations was associated with increased interaction with faculty members and fellow students, growing interest in intellectual and cultural pursuits, greater independence, and liberalization in attitudes. But it was also accompanied by behavior indicating heightened tension and stress and by some feeling of alienation from the college and from fellow students.

Impact on Nonparticipant Students

So far we have looked at some of the consequences of a student's participation in campus demonstrations. But what of the students who did not engage actively in protest, the observers on the sidelines? Did the demonstrations have any significant impact on them? Are men affected differently from women? Are black students affected differently from white students?

The sample used in the analysis to answer these questions consisted of 3261 students who had entered two hundred institutions as freshmen in the fall of 1966 and were followed up three and one-half years later, in the winter of 1969–1970. These students were part of a larger group from which we excluded all respondents who did not indicate that their race was white/Caucasian or black/Negro/Afro-American (that is, we excluded Orientals, American Indians, and "other" racial or ethnic groups). To limit the sample to students who had been exposed to only one institution and who were still in that institution, we also excluded all students who had transferred from or dropped out of their college of matriculation. The final sample consisted of four groups: 1564 white men, 160 black men, 1319 white women, and 218 black women.

Analyses were carried out for each group on forty-two outcome measures (derived from responses to the follow-up questionnaire). The discussion here is limited, however, to outcomes for which the findings seemed meaningful and interpretable. These outcomes are the student's perceptions of the psychological climate or atmosphere of the college, satisfaction with college, political inclinations, and religious preferences. Since we had "pretests" from the SIF on all these variables except satisfaction with college, we could examine changes that had occurred during the college years and thus study the impact of protest occurrence on these outcomes.

The follow-up questionnaire also asked whether the student had helped to organize or lead, participated in, or observed at first hand any demonstration against existing ethnic or racial policies, college administrative policies, or United States military policy. Students who had helped organize or lead demonstrations or had participated in them were regarded as having been involved in protests; those who had merely observed were regarded as nonparticipants. Our focus was primarily on how the occurrence of protest affected this latter group.

To determine how many and what kind of protests had occurred at each of the hundred institutions in the sample, several sources were used: Peterson's (1968a) study for the 1966–1967 academic year; a study by Shoben reported in Foster and Long (1970) for the 1967–1968 academic year; and two ACE surveys for the 1968–1969 and 1969–1970 academic years (Bayer and Astin, 1969; A. Astin, 1971). From these sources, we knew not only what kind of protests (racial, administrative, or antimilitary) had occurred during the three-and-one-half year period but also the number of years in which protests had occurred on a given campus. To get some idea of the severity of a particular protest, we used the arrest of protesters as an index. The three categories of protest were scored 0 to 4, depending on the number of years that the particular event had occurred. In addition, an overall index of total protests was derived simply by adding the three scores for racial, administrative, and antimilitary protests. This index ranged from 0 to 12.

To determine the independent impact of protest occurrence on each of the fourteen outcomes under consideration, we first had to control for three possible sources of bias: student input characteristics, institutional characteristics, and participation in protest. Thus, we again used a series of two-stage regression analyses. In the first, fifty-four student input variables (from the SIF), twenty-one

institutional characteristics, and six participation variables (orga-
nized/led or participated in one of the three categories of protest)
were allowed to enter the regression freely, in stepwise fashion, until
no additional input variable was capable of producing a significant
reduction (p less than .05) in the residual sum of squares. In the
second stage, we were able to isolate the independent effects of the
four occurrence variables (racial protests, administrative protests,
antimilitary protests, and arrests) on the outcomes under consideration. Separate analyses were done for men and women and for
blacks and whites.

The results of the second phase of the series of regression
analyses (partial correlations with nonparticipation) were significant
for four different groups of outcomes: perceptions of the psychological climate of the college, overall satisfaction with the college,
political inclination, and religious preference. The effects on participants (partial correlations with participation as revealed in the first
phase of the analysis) were compared with those on nonparticipants.
In general, students who became involved in a protest as leaders or
as participants were more affected than nonparticipants. For white
men, there were twenty-two significant partial correlations for
participants and sixteen for observers. For white women, there were
seventeen significant correlations for participants and twelve for
observers. Findings for black students of both sexes tended to be
nonsignificant: for black men, there were only three significant
correlations for participants and one for observers; for black women,
there were six significant correlations for participants, four for
observers. Because of the comparatively small size of the black student sample (378, compared to 2883 white students), the correlations required for significance were considerably higher for blacks;
consequently, fewer prediction variables (including participation
variables) entered the regression for blacks, and the number of
significant partial correlations was reduced.

Because of the paucity of findings for blacks, we shall confine
the rest of our summary to white students. The findings on student
perceptions of the college were mixed, in that participation and
observation sometimes had opposing effects. Thus, protesters were
slightly less likely to see the college as liberal, whereas observers
were more apt to say that this adjective was highly descriptive of the

college. Some differences between the sexes appeared. For instance, racial protests had a heavier impact on male participants than on male nonparticipants, but they affected female nonparticipants more than female participants. Administrative protests had a greater effect on female participants and on male nonparticipants. Antimilitary protests affected the perceptions of participants of both sexes more than nonparticipants.

For the outcome of satisfaction with the college experience, administrative protests did not have significant effects on participants or nonparticipants of either sex. Increased satisfaction was associated with racial protests among male observers and with antimilitary protests among female observers, whereas decreased satisfaction for both sexes was even more closely associated with participation in either of these types of protest. One additional finding concerns the effects of the arrest variables: protests that involved arrests were negatively associated with satisfaction among nonparticipants.

Protests—particularly those concerned with racial or war-related issues—had their most profound effects on political and religious preferences. Both observers and participants tended to move toward a more noncomformist position: greater political liberalism and less religious orthodoxy, although the effects were stronger for participants than for observers.

Finally, the findings on political beliefs and satisfaction with college suggest that the one-year effects of participation noted earlier in this chapter are not merely transient phenomena but persist over a much longer period of time (three and one-half years).

This discussion of the effects of the occurrence of protest on both participants and nonparticipants gives us a somewhat longer range view than the results based on a one-year follow-up of freshmen. However, the findings that emerged from these analyses apply primarily to white students.

Not surprisingly, campus demonstrations had a considerable impact on student perceptions of the college, though participants and nonparticipants were affected differently. Nonparticipants became more inclined to regard the college climate as liberal and warm and less inclined to see it as victorian. Moreover, participation in protest tended to decrease a student's satisfaction with college, whereas nonparticipants tended to be more satisfied with their colleges after demonstrations. In short, participants and nonparticipants became more polarized as a result of protest. However, increased political liberalization, the rejection of formal religion, and a shift to no religious preference were consequences of protest for both participants and nonparticipants, though the effect was stronger for participants.

Not only did participants and nonparticipants differ from one another as freshmen (see Chapter Three), but this difference also became wider during the college years as a result of protest. Perhaps while protesters were becoming more caught up in the battle and having their convictions and perceptions reinforced by their association with other protesters, students who did not join demonstrations on their campuses were coming to disfavor campus unrest more and becoming more disturbed by its effects on their institutions and their own college careers.

Overview

In this chapter we have considered the outcomes of protests from two perspectives: impact on the institution, and impact on individuals (administrators, faculty, and students). With respect to the first, our evidence indicates that the majority of institutions across the country implemented significant changes during the peak years of campus unrest (1966–1971). These changes were far-ranging, from curricular revision, greater student representation in governance, and liberalization of parietal rules to alterations in grading systems, hiring of minority group faculty and administrators, and establishment of special admissions policies for minority group students. Few changes were made, however, on war-related issues (such as modification of ROTC programs, elimination of war-related research, and cessation of campus recruiting by certain industries). While many institutions made changes in the absence of protests, changes were much more likely to occur if there was also a related protest. Since these relationships between protests and change held even after student input and institutional characteristics were taken into account, the link seems to be a direct causal one.

Because of the lack of longitudinal data, it was not possible to obtain a definitive picture of the impact of campus unrest on college administrators. Our interviews with beleaguered administrators, however, did reveal a consistent perception. While they generally agreed that protests had resulted in certain positive changes (particularly in the areas of governance and curricular reform), administrators also felt that demonstrations had had an adverse effect on their own lives.

In order to assess the impact of protests on students, we found it necessary to separate participants from observers. As might be expected, participation in campus protests was associated with more far-ranging changes than mere observation. Protest participation was, first of all, associated with a generally increased level of activity: greater interaction with teachers and fellow students, increased reading, more frequent participation in artistic and cultural activities, and increased use of alcohol, cigarettes, and tranquilizers. The last three items suggest that participation was also associated with a greater anxiety and stress.

In terms of student attitudes and beliefs, participation was associated with a move toward the left of the political spectrum. In addition, participation in a particular type of protest was associated with a strengthening of attitudes related to that issue. Thus, participation in a student power protest was associated with a strengthening of the belief that students should be given more power in decision-making. Likewise, participation in a racial protest was associated with a strengthening of the belief that disadvantaged students should be given preferential treatment.

Demonstrations had a somewhat different pattern of effects on nonparticipant observers. Protests seemed to strengthen the nonparticipants' belief that the campus atmosphere was liberal rather than Victorian. Although protest participation was associated with increasing student dissatisfaction with college, protests did not generally affect the degree of satisfaction expressed by nonparticipants. However, extreme protests in which arrests occurred tended to have a negative effect on nonparticipants' satisfaction with college.

The only areas in which protests appeared to have parallel effects on both participants and nonparticipants were political and religious beliefs. For both groups, protests were associated with a move toward the left of the political spectrum and a secularizing of religious beliefs.

VII

PRESENT
AND FUTURE
REPERCUSSIONS

To examine the legacy of campus unrest and change, we first review the highlights of our empirical studies. What has been learned
about the impact of campus protests on the individuals involved and
on institutional policies and practices? We extend this evidence by
presenting recent national survey data comparing college students
with those who attended during the peak years of campus unrest.
Are the values expressed by these earlier students shared by students
today? In light of these findings, we discuss the current campus
"calm" and offer a brief commentary on current protests. We conclude with an admittedly speculative analysis of the future of campus unrest.

Highlights of Empirical Findings

Our analyses of the etiology of protest show clearly that
campus protests arose because of a variety of factors. Protests during
the late 1960s and early 1970s were not, as some social analysts

might have us believe, nearly universal phenomena that swept most of our campuses with equal frequency, intensity, and violence. Many campuses were virtually untouched by student unrest, many had several incidents of protests, and a few—those frequently reported in the national news media—had a continuing series of severe and sometimes violent protests.

The occurrence of unrest on a particular campus was clearly not a random event; rather, there were identifiable antecedent conditions that influenced the likelihood that protests would develop. Contrary to the rhetoric of some protesters, however, the occurrence of certain types of protests on a given campus depended less on the specific policies and practices of that institution than on the characteristics of its student body and faculty. Indeed, liberalness or permissiveness in the administrative policies of an institution made protests more likely to occur, if anything. However, the effect of this factor was small in comparison to the effects of student and faculty attributes.

The faculty and student attributes associated with the emergence of campus protests and with participation in or support of protests have a number of common elements: either being Jewish or having no religious preference, having liberal or left political beliefs, and being interested in the humanities or social sciences. These attributes are associated with participation in all types of protests, but most strongly with participation in war-related protests. Being black is strongly associated with participation in protests about racial issues, is moderately associated with protesting about institutional administrative policies, and shows no relation to participation in war-related protests.

Once the personal characteristics of students and faculty are taken into account, the institutional characteristic most consistently associated with the emergence of protest is size. At least two (not necessarily contradictory) explanations for this association are possible. The "critical mass" hypothesis states simply that, the larger the enrollment of a college, the more likely it will be to have a sufficient number of protest-oriented students to organize an effective demonstration. The second explanation is that larger institutions—particularly research-oriented universities—typically have impersonal environments in which relatively little concern is shown for the individual student; the resulting student alienation and lack of commitment to the institution increase the likelihood that students will participate in demonstrations. Our study has provided at least partial support for both interpretations.

Whether or not a student becomes involved in campus demonstrations also depends on certain environmental contingencies. Thus, the student's chances of participating are maximized if he or she lives on campus rather than at home, associates primarily with students in the humanities or social sciences, and does not join a social fraternity or sorority. (Use of marijuana and LSD is also strongly associated with participation in demonstrations but our data are ambiguous about the direction of causation.)

While living on campus obviously provides the student with greater opportunity to be present at demonstrations, other evidence suggests that this effect on protest behavior may be mediated by a change in political attitudes that also accompanies campus residence.

Once a protest begins, the course it follows and the changes it brings about depend on a number of factors: the issues, the participants, the tactics used, and the character of the administrative response. While some critics of the student movement have alleged that police have to be brought on campus to quell the violence that results from demonstrations, our data show clearly that the presence of police is a stimulus to, rather than an antidote for, physical violence. The most productive form of administrative response to protests appears to be a willingness to discuss the specific demands of protesters. Administrations have been particularly willing to discuss the demands of black students, but showed little willingness to discuss the demands of antiwar protesters.

Protests led by black students and those supported by the student government most often achieved at least some of their objectives. Considering the great amount of attention received by SDS and related radical left organizations, it is perhaps remarkable that they so often proved ineffective in their attempts to bring about change through protest activity. On the other hand, it could be argued that the protest activities of these organizations, which were often well publicized by the news media, helped to sensitize others to certain issues and to create a national climate in which people in general were more likely to engage in some form of protest activity.

Our analysis of the outcomes of campus protests suggests that campus unrest had widespread and often profound effects on the programs and governance of many institutions. Many of these changes are now institutionalized. During the peak period of protest activity (1966–1971), a majority of the institutions across the country implemented significant changes in their programs and policies. These included curricular revisions and introduction of new programs (particularly ethnic studies), formation of new committees or study groups, granting greater student representation on existing committees, establishment of special admissions policies for minority group students, liberalization of parietal rules, reforms in the judicial process, alterations in the grading system and in graduation requirements, and hiring more black faculty or administrators. Few changes, however, were made with respect to war-related policies or programs (ROTC, military research, recruiting on campus by war-related industries and the armed services). While many changes were made in the absence of protest, our longitudinal studies indicate that, in many instances, changes can be directly attributable to the occurrence of protests on the campus. In other words, protests, particularly those on non-war-related issues, very often tended to "work."

Since changes that were introduced in the absence of protests could be interpreted as strategic gestures designed to head off possible protests, one could argue that these changes were an indirect effect of protests occurring elsewhere. Whatever the objectives of these gratuitous changes, our longitudinal analysis shows that, when an institution introduced a change without a protest, no related protest was likely to occur. This finding may mean that when an institution introduces a change without the pressure of protest, it preempts the students' demands without giving them a sense of victory that might lead them to press for further concessions. At the same time, the national climate of unrest—created by its prevalence on other campuses—was probably an important determinant of institutional change on campuses where no unrest occurred. While our study was not addressed specifically to these "epidemiological" aspects of protests, it seems likely that the news media played a key role in contributing to the spread of unrest from campus to campus.

With respect to the effects of protests on students, it was

possible for us to examine short-term changes only. It is understandable that the occurrence of campus protests had more striking effects on participants than on observers. Participating in demonstrations was associated with increased liberalization in students' political attitudes and values, greater interaction among students and between students and faculty, increased student interest in intellectual and cultural pursuits, and greater student independence. At the same time, participation seemed to be accompanied by increased tension and stress and greater feelings of alienation from college and from fellow students.

Students who observed a protest on their campus seemed to become more inclined to view their college as liberal and friendly. Not surprisingly, the attitudes of students about how to deal with protests became more polarized when a protest occurred. Bystanders became more inclined to feel the administrators were too lax on protesters, whereas protest participants developed the opposite point of view. Both nonparticipants and participants, however, appeared to become more liberal in their religious and political attitudes and convictions as a consequence of protests.

Students Today

The relative calm prevailing on college campuses during the mid-1970s has prompted many journalists and pundits to suggest that college students today are less committed to social issues and more conservative than students who attended college during the peak years of campus unrest. Such claims imply that one legacy of the student movement has been withdrawal of students from involvement in social issues and a return to the behavior of the "silent generation" of the 1950s.

What are the facts? Are students today different from their predecessors a few years ago? If so, in what ways have their attitudes toward major political, social, and campus issues altered? Are definite trends or shifts discernible?

Most recent studies of student attitudes are restricted in their generalizability because they are either based on relatively small numbers or limited to a single institution. Many focus on only a single social issue rather than a broad range of issues, and most do not include time series data. We were fortunate, therefore, in having access to the results of an ongoing large-scale, nationally representative survey of students that provides time series data on attitudes for a broad array of issues.

Each fall since 1966 the Cooperative Institutional Research Program (CIRP) has surveyed a representative national sample of approximately three hundred thousand entering freshmen at some three hundred institutions (two- and four-year colleges and universities) throughout the nation. Student responses are statistically weighted to represent the total population of entering college students, and annual normative data are reported (Astin, King, and others, 1974).

Since 1967, the CIRP questionnaire has asked students for their opinions on a number of political, national, and campus issues. These questions have varied somewhat over the years; some items have been added, others have been dropped and then reintroduced. More than fifty different substantive issues have been addressed at least once in the CIRP surveys since 1967. Data will be presented here for only those twenty attitudinal items in which data are available for at least three different years.

We shall examine recent changes in students' political self-identification and trends in students' positions on specific controversial issues concerning the campus and the society.

Political Identification. Students were first asked to indicate their political identification in the 1969 CIRP survey. A similar question has been included in each annual survey since that time, although the response categories were changed in 1970 to provide better response symmetry, and minor format changes were introduced in 1971 and 1972. Despite these alterations, a trend is clearly discernible between the late 1960s and the mid-1970s.

In the six years for which data are available (1969–1974), there has been a steady convergence from both ends of the political spectrum to the political center. Fewer students are inclined to take a positive political stance, and the proportion endorsing a middle-of-the-road position has increased from 44 percent in 1969 to 55 percent in 1974.

Most of the shift since 1969 has occurred from the right (conservative and far right). One-third fewer students are found on the right side of the political spectrum in 1974, while the left (liberal and far left) has lost less than one-tenth. However, if one takes 1970 as a starting point (probably a more valid one, since the item alternatives have remained the same since then), the relative declines through 1974 are almost identical: about 18 percent from both left and right. In each year through 1974, liberals outnumbered conservatives by about two to one, and far left students outnumbered far right students by about three to one. Thus, the overall left-right orientation of students has not shifted appreciably since the peak years of campus unrest.

These results suggest neither increased liberalism nor increased conservativism among successive new cohorts of college students. Rather, the convergence toward the center could be characterized as a kind of political "depolarization" of college students in the mid-1970s. It must be stressed, however, that these political labels are probably relative rather than absolute. What might have been characterized only a few years ago as a "liberal" position on certain issues (women's rights, for example), may now be perceived as the "mainstream" position.

Societal Views. The CIRP attitudinal items covered eight general categories of social issues: women, population control, desegregation, the environment, consumer protection, economic equity, crime, and drugs. One of the more substantial shifts in student opinion was on the traditional role of women, no doubt a reflection in part of the impact of the women's liberation movement on student attitudes. In 1967, the first year in which the item was included, well over half the entering freshmen favored a conventional role for women. Endorsement of this item has declined steadily since that time, with fewer than 30 percent of all students favoring this view in 1974. These changes have continued since the decline of campus unrest; indeed, the largest change—in both absolute and relative terms—occurred between 1972 and 1973, well after major unrest had disappeared from American campuses. Effects of the women's movement are also reflected in the increased proportion of entering college freshmen who favor full job equality for women. In 1970, eight out of ten freshmen endorsed equal salaries and opportunities for women; fully nine out of ten since 1972 have supported the same position.

An item assessing student awareness of the population problem growth and support for population control was also included in the 1967 survey and has been repeated in recent surveys. In 1967, only 42 percent endorsed programs to discourage large families; by 1971, 68 percent supported such programs. Since 1971, the proportion has declined somewhat (to 60 percent in 1974), although current support for population control is still well above that of the 1960s.

Student positions on school desegregation were measured in three consecutive surveys (1971, 1972, and 1973). Results indicate that student opinion in the early 1970s was about equally divided on whether the federal government was doing enough to promote school desegregation. Only minor fluctuations in the proportion endorsing this issue are apparent, and no definite trend is discernible.

With respect to the environment, a substantial majority of students believe that not enough is being done to control pollution. In 1971, over 90 percent of the students agreed with this view. The proportion has declined steadily since then to 83 percent of the 1974 freshmen. However, here, as in several other attitudinal items in the CIRP surveys, the same wording may have a different meaning at different times. Since the turn of the decade, substantial (and controversial) antipollution regulations have been implemented—most notably automobile emission controls and air emission standards for industry. Despite several negative factors—publicity criticizing some of these policies, added consumer costs resulting from increased prices and greater energy consumption, and the need to use more expensive, higher quality energy resources to meet emission standards—the vast majority of young people entering college in 1974 still endorsed stronger regulatory activity than that currently mandated by the federal government.

Greater consumer protection by the federal government is likewise endorsed by a majority of students, and this view has changed little in recent years. Fully three-fourths of each freshman class in the past four years have agreed that not enough is being done to protect the consumer from faulty goods and services.

Two attitudinal items address issues of economic equity in the United States. While data for both items are limited to a relatively recent period and hence provide minimal information for judging possible trends since the campus unrest era, they suggest a small increase in support of greater economic equity. In 1972, 73 percent of freshmen believed that the wealthy should pay a larger share of taxes, compared to 76 percent in 1974. A much more radical egalitarian statement—that people should be paid equally for hard work regardless of their ability or the quality of their work—received the support of 25 percent of the students in 1972 and increased slightly to 28 percent in 1974. These short-term data clearly do not support the hypothesis that students have recently shifted toward greater conservatism on economic issues.

The CIRP items on crime and the courts likewise show little change over the same time period. Approximately half the freshmen entering college during the first half of the 1970s agreed that "there is too much concern in the courts for the rights of criminals." In the six years for which data are available on this item, the highest levels of endorsement (in other words, the most conservative responses) are found in the earlier years, but the change has been relatively slight. Similarly, in the three years (1969, 1970, and 1971) when students were queried about capital punishment, there was a slight increase (from 54 percent to 58 percent) in the proportion endorsing abolishment of the death penalty.

One of the most pronounced trends in attitudes concerned the marijuana laws. Since 1968, the first year in which an item on this subject was included in the survey, the proportion of freshmen who agreed that marijuana should be legalized has more than doubled. In 1968, one-fifth of the entering freshmen thought so; in 1969, one-fourth; in 1970 and 1971 almost two-fifths; and in the last three years the proportion appears to have stabilized at slightly less than half.

Campus Views. Nine attitudinal items on campus issues from the CIRP surveys met the criteria for inclusion in the present analyses. They fall into five general areas: student jurisdiction, administrative jurisdiction, admissions policy, grading practice, and athletic policy.

An item on student evaluations of faculty has been included in each CIRP survey since 1967. From 1967 through 1972 there was a regular increase in the proportion of freshmen who agreed that faculty promotions should be based in part on student evaluations. In 1972, fully three-fourths of the students endorsed this position.

The two most recent years showed a slight reversal, dropping to 74 percent in 1974. Nevertheless, substantially more students in the mid-1970s than the late 1960s believed they should have a voice in their instructors' advancement.

Four items on administrative responsibility were included in virtually all CIRP surveys. Without exception, each reflected increasing support from the mid-1960s to the mid-1970s for restricting the purview of academic administrators, although the data from the last several years suggest a leveling off in the trend. In the 1967–1968 period, approximately half the freshmen agreed that student publications should be cleared by college officials and that college officials were too lax in dealing with student protesters; by the mid-1970s only about a third were endorsing the same statements. In the latter part of the 1960s about one-third agreed that college officials had the right to ban certain speakers from the campus, compared to less than one-fourth in the mid-1970s. With respect to regulating students' off-campus behavior, 23 percent of the 1968 freshmen thought this a legitimate activity of college officials, compared to only 14 percent in 1974.

One of the few indications of a conservative trend, albeit slight, is the change in student attitudes on giving preferential treatment in college admissions to students from disadvantaged backgrounds. Since the late 1960s, the proportion of students endorsing this item has declined about 5 percent (from about 43 percent to 38 percent). Counterindication of any overall conservative trend on admissions issues, however, is provided by the increased support for open admissions. In 1971, 37 percent approved of this policy; in the most recent year for which data are available (1974), the figure was 40 percent.

The only other indication of growing support for traditional academic procedures concerns grading practices. At the turn of the decade, a surprisingly high proportion of freshmen (44 percent) thought that the grading system should be abolished. There has been a regular decline in support for this proposal each successive year, with only 29 percent of the 1974 college entrants endorsing this position. Several factors may be involved here: the end of the draft (and of draft deferments), and the recent relaxation in grading standards at both secondary and postsecondary levels.

A growing minority of students support deemphasis of collegiate sports. In the earliest survey year (1967), only 21 percent agreed that colleges would be improved if organized sports were deemphasized; in 1974, this proportion had grown to 28 percent.

Conclusions. The popular characterization of students of the mid-1970s as being more apathetic, more conservative, and less socially conscious than their predecessors during the 1960s gains little support from our comparative analysis of trends in student opinion. While incidents of massive student protests, widely publicized in the 1960s, have apparently declined in frequency, the relatively high proportion of current students endorsing liberal positions (as compared to student generations of the 1960s) is strong evidence that changes in student attitudes and beliefs that occurred during the 1960s have persisted well into the 1970s. While students are increasingly likely to describe themselves as "middle-of-the-road" politically, they continue to take positions on social issues that would have been described only a few years ago as "liberal."

In short, the gradual convergence toward a noncommittal political stance ("depolarization") that appears from the late 1960s to the mid-1970s has been accompanied by consistent increases in student support for most liberal societal and collegiate issues and policies. Apparently, one legacy of campus unrest is that yesterday's "liberal" views have become today's "mainstream" views.

The relatively high level of awareness and concern about social and college issues shown by the most recent college entrants indicates that the campus is likely to continue to be a strong locus of support for social reform. Moreover, research on changes in student attitudes that occur after entering college (see Chapter Six; A. Astin, 1972; Feldman and Newcomb, 1969) indicates that the liberalizing trend observed recently in successive classes of entering freshmen is reinforced by changes within each class during the undergraduate years. Thus, college students today display a potential for active involvement in social causes and social reform that is every bit as great as that manifested more concretely by their predecessors in the late 1960s.

Of all the changes in student attitudes that constitute part of the legacy of campus unrest, perhaps the most significant are those associated with women's rights and the role of women in

society. Indeed, it is difficult not to view the women's movement at
least in part as an outgrowth of campus unrest. In much the same
way that the antiwar movement grew out of the civil rights movement, the student movement provided a context for the evolution
of this new major protest movement. This is not to suggest that the
women's movement would not have occurred in the absence of
campus unrest, but rather that its development was facilitated
by the climate of protest and the array of tactical approaches and
strategies that characterized the student movement. Furthermore,
while the antiwar aspect of campus unrest was a transitory phenomenon (which may, of course, reappear in the event of future
wars), the women's movement is generating a series of societal
changes that are presumably much more permanent and pervasive.
Thus, the trends reflected in the attitudinal items concerning
women's roles and rights are not likely ever to be reversed.

Decline of Campus Activism

The three case studies reported in Chapter Five give the
impression that the climate of the typical institution during the
mid-1970s is radically different from that during the height of protest activities (1966 to 1971). Each case study portrays a campus
environment characterized by an aura of tension, excitement, antici-
pation, involvement, and social concern. Many students and faculty
apparently felt they were participants in, or at least observers of,
events of profound social significance. Whether or not campuses will
ever return to such a state in the future is difficult to predict.

It is tempting to conclude that the premature claims of
"eerie tranquillity" on college campuses that were made in the early
1970s became a kind of self-fulfilling prophecy for the mid-1970s.
Even though these claims were made in a context of considerable
activism, the fact that they were widely accepted as accurate may
have been a signal to students that political unrest was passé. While
there may be some truth in this assumption, our study indicates that
other factors have contributed more significantly to the dramatic
decline in campus unrest.

Disappearance of Major Issues. Perhaps the most critical

factor in the decline of campus activism has been the disappearance of viable issues. Our longitudinal analyses (Chapters Three to Six) show clearly that whether institutions experienced protests, which students got involved, and what outcomes occurred were highly dependent on the issues underlying the protest. We have classified these issues in three general categories: antiwar, racial, and campus life (including governance). Except for the antiwar protests, the demonstrations tended to produce changes on the issues concerned. In short, protests were frequently successful in their aims. And, as we have noted, institutions that did not experience protests frequently undertook some of the same changes in governance, campus life, and racial issues that were the objectives of protests on other campuses.

Although they were sometimes hard-won, changes in campus policy with respect to blacks were substantial and pervasive. Most institutions undertook serious campaigns to recruit minority students, faculty, and staff. Many colleges actually established black studies programs, African studies institutes, and black-oriented courses in the basic disciplines. Black student organizations were accorded greater legitimacy and status, and in a few cases attempts at establishing black dormitories or black-oriented sections of dormitories were undertaken. Clearly, the actions of many institutions have alleviated the concerns that underpinned most racial protests during the late 1960s and early 1970s.

In the area of campus life and governance, too, many issues have been assuaged by the actions of institutions. Parietal rules, for example, are a thing of the past on most campuses. Students have been granted considerable freedom of action in the areas of sexual behavior, drinking, and scheduling of their own time and activities. Many institutions have even assumed a hands-off position on the issue of drug use, leaving the matter entirely to the civil authorities, whose presence on campuses is typically discouraged.

With respect to campus governance, it is now standard procedure on many campuses to have student representatives on key committees and, in a few instances, on boards of trustees. When students are not represented or are nonvoting members, their advice is often sought as a routine matter. Censorship of campus publications is either minimal or nonexistent. The student judicial process is controlled primarily or exclusively by the students on many campuses.

Changes in academic matters have perhaps been less dramatic, probably because student protests tended to focus on personal freedom and governance more than on academic issues. Nevertheless, there have been attempts at modification of grading systems (the pass-fail option, for example) and greater attention is being paid to student ratings of instruction. Student leaves of absence are formally sanctioned and even encouraged on some campuses.

While our research shows that campuses seldom changed their policies and practices about war-related issues, the viability of these issues has been undermined by changes in national policy. Unquestionably, the most critical of these changes was the winding down of United States involvement in the war in Southeast Asia and the eventual collapse of regimes supported by the United States. In addition, the draft has been ended, a nuclear test ban treaty has been signed with the Soviet Union, weapons of biological warfare have been banned, and a political détente with mainland China has been achieved.

Other Factors. While our analysis suggests strongly that the decline of campus unrest reflects the disappearance or alleviation of the underlying issues, rather than a change in the basic values and aspirations of students, there are a number of other possible contributory factors.

Some observers have suggested that much of the energy of the new left has been siphoned away from issues of racism and militarism and redirected into the women's liberation movement. Indeed, the student left of the 1960s has been viewed by some as basically sexist, with leadership roles assumed by men and subordinate roles (either as support staff or as sex objects) by women. Whether or not this view is accurate, neither the antiwar movement nor the black movement could likely be sustained for very long if the women were to withdraw. While our data do not offer any definitive tests of this hypothesis, the data on consecutive freshman classes discussed above in this chapter show clearly that there was a dramatic change between 1969 and 1973 in the attitudes of both sexes toward the role of women and toward equal rights for women.

These trends suggest that the women's movement has drawn increasing support from students of both sexes during the past few years and therefore represents an increasingly serious competitor for the energies of activists. Activist women today are probably not inclined to attach themselves to causes that do not involve some aspect of the women's movement.

Several sources cite disenchantment with radical activism as a factor in the decline of campus unrest. One view is that students who might otherwise have been sympathetic with the issues were repelled by the excesses of the radical left. Another version is that students, including many on the left, became convinced that radical campus activity was ineffective in bringing about real changes, and they therefore turned to other channels (the traditional political process, for example). Our data suggest that neither view is a major factor in the decline of activism on the campus. One fact revealed by our consecutive years of data from entering freshmen is that students have not defected in large numbers from the left side of the political spectrum; rather, the left-right balance has remained fairly stable. Nor has there been any tendency by students to back away from commitment to basic social issues that are normally identified with the left. There is, in short, no evidence of a "disenchantment" with the left. By the same token, our data (Chapters Four, Five, and Six, in particular) suggest that campus protests often did work. And even though individual institutions generally failed to respond to war-related protests, dramatic changes in national policy on these issues did occur. This is not to say, of course, that those on the radical left are entirely satisfied with the changes and no longer feel the need for revolutionary activity, but simply that many of the specific changes sought through protests were in fact made, and very often in direct response to protest activity.

Since the decline of campus unrest was accompanied by (or perhaps slightly preceded by) a decline in public support for higher education and by an increasingly tight job market for college graduates, it has been suggested that students have turned away from campus activism as a result of growing concern about their economic welfare and eventual career prospects. Again, while no definitive test of this assumption is available at this time, national data do not reveal any pronounced shifts either in the degree of concern shown by college students about job security or in their orientation toward careers that offer relatively more security (Astin, King, and others, 1974).

Some critics on the left attribute the decline in campus activism to what they describe as the repressive measures used by institutions and governments to stifle unrest. They argue that repressive measures grew to the point where students were sufficiently frightened or intimidated to decline to participate in protests. Examples of such repressive measures would be the indiscriminate use of force to quell protests, the enactment of punitive legislation by many state legislatures, and the hard line taken by prominent public figures (former Vice-President Agnew being perhaps the most well-known critic). This particular interpretation, however, receives very little support from our data. If anything, our analysis of the dynamics of protests (Chapter Four) suggests that excessive use of force may prolong protests or even lead to additional protests. The most extreme examples of repression (the killing of students at Jackson State and Kent State, for example) precipitated some of the most widespread protests. Also, it appears that the inclination to use outside police and the readiness of police to use force indiscriminately gradually tempered during the most active years of campus unrest. In short, the repression theory gains very little support from our data.

Some attribute the decline of campus unrest to a redirection of student energy. This interpretation is similar to that based on the women's movement. Supporters of "redirection" theories contend that the ecology movement and various religious movements have drawn away and redirected the energies of many students. That the environment is an issue paramount in the minds of many students is supported by the consecutive surveys of entering freshmen. As a matter of fact, the Earth Day demonstrations (see Chapter One) were more widespread and involved more institutions than any other single protest event. (A critical difference, of course, is that the Earth Day protests were not directed against the institutions.) Other factors cited as competing for the student's time and energy are transcendental meditation, yoga, spiritualism, organizations of "Jesus freaks," and massage. Of course, increased student interest in such phenomena might be more a result than a cause of the decline in political activities.

Campus Protest Today

While our data do not permit a systematic statistical study of the extent of campus unrest nationally after 1971–1972, a cursory look at campuses during the mid-1970s does not support the widely accepted assumption that campus unrest is a thing of the past. For example, the following is a sampling of campus protests reported in the news media during the spring of 1975.

University of California at Santa Barbara: takeover of campus computer by students demanding continued funding of Chicano and black studies center, recruitment of more minorities, and resignation of chancellor, affirmative action coordinator, and newspaper editor (twenty-five students arrested).

Siena Heights College: one-day student strike over student services and academic program.

Duke University: demonstration by six hundred students over proposal to phase out school of forestry and primate research.

Iowa State University: student boycott of political science classes over failure to rehire instructor because of nonpublication.

San Francisco State University: occupation of building by one hundred students to prevent address by Nazi party leaders (fighting; two persons injured).

Brown University: student strike voted (2956 to 763) in opposition to proposed cuts in scholarships and programs for black students. Sixty minority students occupy administration building for thirty-eight hours, while one hundred to one hundred fifty picket outside.

University of California at Los Angeles: two hundred students demonstrate for greater control of ethnic studies programs by minority students.

Bryant College: one-week boycott of classes by students in support of strike by campus maintenance workers.

Massachusetts Institute of Technology: students vote (8870 to 1031) to boycott classes for two days to protest proposed budget reductions (including cuts in special minority programs).

State University of New York at Buffalo: one hundred persons occupy building to protest ban on use of student funds to transport students to rally for defendents in Attica prison riot (ten students arrested; four security officers injured).

Massachusetts Institute of Technology: one hundred persons stage sit-in to protest university agreement to train engineers for Iran (issue: risk of proliferation of nuclear power).

Brandeis University: students picket and occupy building to protest proposed budget cuts in special programs for minority students.

In most respects these items are identical to those that received widespread press coverage during the late 1960s. If nothing else, they suggest that campuses today are far from quiescent and that issues of academic programs, minority concerns, and student rights will continue to provide a basis for student protests in the future.

Future of Campus Unrest and Change

If our notion about the centrality of issues is correct, there is a real possibility that widespread campus unrest will reappear if a new set of issues arises. Our data on the most recent classes of college freshmen suggest that students today are just as "protest-prone" as those a few years ago. Given new issues, the current generation of college students might well be capable of engaging in widespread protest behavior. Considering the apparent importance of faculty involvement, as revealed in Chapters Three and Four, the fact that many of the demonstrators of the 1960s are or will soon be college faculty members reinforces the conclusion that campuses today and in the immediate future have the potential for a high level of unrest.

It is interesting to speculate on the courses future protests might take. The equivocal nature of many changes in campus life, particularly in the academic area, suggests that viable issues may still be uncovered and identified. College admissions practices, for example, have received little attention (except in terms of minority admissions). Another issue is the quality of teaching and the related question of research versus teaching. Protests still arise occasionally on the issue of tenure, particularly for faculty members who do not publish but who are regarded by students as good teachers.

Still another group of issues deals with credentials and the availability of jobs. If the job market for college graduates continues to tighten and if admissions criteria for graduate and professional schools become more stringent, the adequacy of job counseling and placement and the appropriateness of curricula to the world of work may become viable undergraduate issues. The interface between higher education and the military-industrial complex was, of course, one of the key issues in war-related protests. The interface between higher education and the world of work, and the more general question of the relationship between education and the economy, might prove fertile grounds for protest issues in the future.

In spite of the many concessions granted by institutions as a result of racial protests, the economic and educational problems of black and other minorities (especially Spanish-speaking and Native American) are far from solved. While some may argue that higher education has done all it can reasonably be expected to do for these ethnic minorities, there are still many unresolved issues that could invoke a new round of racial protests on college campuses. Financing of minority programs is already a protest issue on many campuses, particularly in light of the budget squeeze affecting most institutions. Admissions policies present still another problem. In spite of the recruitment efforts of many institutions, the proportion of minority students enrolling in colleges and universities is still substantially below the proportion in the population, and enrollment is even showing signs of tapering off (Astin, King, and others, 1974). While the data for admissions to graduate and professional schools are not as reliable, there is reason to believe that ethnic minorities are even more poorly represented there, particularly with recent reductions in federal support for graduate students, which result in a tightening of admissions standards. Then there is the related problem of "tracking." Many public systems of higher education continue to allocate students to different types of institutions on the basis of the traditional criteria of high school grades and scores on tests of academic ability. Since the investment of public funds in the different institutions is far from equal, and since there is reason to believe that the resulting benefits to students may also be unequal (A. Astin, 1972, 1975), the admissions sorting process may well become a major issue for protest activity on the campus.

Just which issues will predominate and whether any will develop in the near future to the intensity experienced in the late 1960s are difficult to predict. Suffice it to say that many issues remain unresolved and that campus unrest, in one form or another, is likely to persist as a symptom of these issues for a long time to come.

BIBLIOGRAPHY

"A Declaration on Campus Unrest." *Educational Record,* Spring 1969, *50,* 144–146.

ATLBACH, P., AND PETERSON, P. "Before Berkeley: Historical Perspectives on American Student Activism." *Annals of the American Academy of Political and Social Science,* May 1971, *395,* 1–14.

"A Statement on Confidentiality, Use of Results, and Independence." *Science,* July 11, 1969.

ASTIN, A. W. "A Program of Research on Student Development." *Journal of College Student Personnel,* 1968, 299–307.

ASTIN, A. W. "New Evidence on Campus Unrest, 1969–70." *Educational Record,* Winter 1971, *52.*

ASTIN, A. W. "The Measured Effects of Higher Education." *The Annals of the American Academy of Political and Social Science,* Nov. 1972, *404,* 1–20.

ASTIN, A. W. *Preventing Students from Dropping Out.* San Francisco: Jossey-Bass, 1975.

ASTIN, A. W., AND BAYER, A. E. "Antecedents and Consequents of Disruptive Campus Protests." *Measurement and Evaluation in Guidance,* Apr. 1971, *4,* 18–30.

ASTIN, A. W., AND BORUCH, R. F. "A 'Link' System for Assuring Confidentiality of Research Data in Longitudinal Studies." *American Educational Research Journal,* Nov. 1970, *7.*

ASTIN, A. W., KING, M. R., LIGHT, J. M., AND RICHARDSON, G. T. *The*

American Freshman: National Norms for Fall 1974. Los Angeles: Graduate School of Education, University of California, 1974.

ASTIN, H. S. "Self-Perceptions of College Student Activists." *Journal of College Student Personnel,* 1971, *12* (4).

ASTIN, H. S., BISCONTI, A. S., HERMAN, M., AND HOFRICHTER, R. *Themes and Events of Campus Unrest in Twenty-Two Colleges and Universities.* Washington, D.C.: Bureau of Social Science Research, 1969.

BAY, C. "Political and Apolitical Students: Facts in Search of Theory." *Journal of Social Issues,* 1967, *23,* 76–91.

BAYER, A. E. *College and University Faculty: A Statistical Description.* ACE Research Reports, Vol. 5, No. 5. Washington, D.C.: American Council on Education, 1970.

BAYER, A. E. *Institutional Correlates of Faculty Support of Campus Unrest.* ACE Research Reports, Vol. 6, No. 1. Washington, D.C.: American Council on Education, 1971.

BAYER, A. E., AND ASTIN, A. W. "Violence and Disruption on the U.S. Campus, 1968–69." *Educational Record,* fall 1969, *50,* 337–350.

BAYER, A. E., AND ASTIN, A. W. "Campus Unrest: Was It Really All That Quiet?" *Educational Record,* fall 1971, *52,* 301–313.

BAYER, A. E., AND ASTIN, A. W. *War Protests on U.S. Campuses during April 1972.* ACE Higher Education Panel Report No. 9. Washington, D.C.: American Council on Education, May 1972.

BAYER, A. E., ASTIN, A. W., AND BORUCH, R. F. *Social Issues and Protest Activity: Recent Student Trends.* ACE Research Reports, Vol. 5, No. 2. Washington, D.C.: American Council on Education, 1970.

BAYER, A. E., ASTIN, A. W., AND BORUCH, R. F. "College Students' Attitudes toward Social Issues: 1967–70." *Educational Record,* winter 1971, *52,* 52–59.

BAYER, A. E., AND DUTTON, J. E. *Trends in Attitudes on Political, Social, and Collegiate Issues among College Students: The Mid-1960s to Mid-1970.* Paper presented at the annual meeting of the American College Personnel Association. Atlanta, Ga., Mar. 1975.

BELL, D. "Columbia and the New Left." In D. Bell and I. Kirstol (Eds.), *Confrontation.* New York: Basic Books, 1968.

BISCONTI, A. S., AND ASTIN, A. W. *The Dynamics of Protest.* Los Angeles: Laboratory for Research on Higher Education, Graduate School of Education, University of California, 1973.

BORUCH, R. F., AND CREAGER, J. A. *Measurement Error in Social and Educational Survey Research.* ACE Research Reports, Vol. 7, No. 2. Washington, D.C.: American Council on Education, 1972.

BUNZEL, J. H. "Costs of Politicized College." *Educational Record,* spring 1969, *50,* 131.

CHICKERING, A. W. *Commuters Versus Resident Students: Overcoming the Educational Inequities of Living Off Campus.* San Francisco: Jossey-Bass, 1974.

COHEN, M. *Guns on Campus: Student Protest at Cornell.* Chicago: Urban Research Corporation, 1970.

CREAGER, J. A. *General Purpose Sampling in the Domain of Higher Education.* ACE Research Reports, Vol. 3, No. 2. Washington, D.C.: American Council on Education, 1968.

CREAGER, J. A. *Test–Retest Statistics and Reliabilities for Reported Attitudes about Campus and Social Issues.* Mimeographed. Washington, D.C.: American Council on Education, 1970.

CREAGER, J. A. *The American Graduate Student: A Normative Description.* ACE Research Reports, Vol. 6, No. 5. Washington, D.C.: American Council on Education, 1971.

CREAGER, J. A., AND SELL, C. L. *The Institutional Domain of Higher Education: A Characteristics File for Research.* ACE Research Reports, Vol. 4, No. 6. Washington, D.C.: American Council on Education, 1969.

FELDMAN, K. A., AND NEWCOMB, T. M. *The Impact of College on Students.* San Francisco: Jossey-Bass, 1969.

FLACKS, R. "The Liberated Generation: An Exploration of the Roots of Student Protest." *Journal of Social Issues,* 1967, *23,* 52–75.

"Fold, Spindle, and Mutilate." *Columbia Daily Spectator,* Jan.. 6, 1970.

FOSTER, J. F. S., AND LONG, D. *Protest! Student Activism in America.* New York: Morrow, 1970.

GADDY, D. *The Scope of Organized Student Protest in Junior Colleges.* Washington, D.C.: American Association of Junior Colleges, 1970.

GLAZER, N. *Remembering the Answers: Essays on the American Student Revolt.* New York: Basic Books, 1970.

GOUGH, H. G., AND HEILBRUN, A. B., JR. *Manual for the Adjective Check List.* Stanford, Calif.: Consulting Psychologists Press, 1965.

HODGKINSON, H. L. "Student Protest—An Institutional and National Profile." *Teachers College Record,* 1970a, *71,* 537–555.

HODGKINSON, H. L. *Institutions in Transition: A Study of Change in*

Higher Education. Berkeley: Carnegie Commission on Higher Education, 1970b.

KATZ, J., AND ASSOCIATES. *No Time for Youth: Growth and Constraint in College Students.* San Francisco: Jossey-Bass, 1968.

KENISTON, K. *Young Radicals: Notes on Committed Youth.* New York: Harcourt Brace Jovanovich, 1968.

KENISTON, K. *Youth and Dissent.* New York: Harcourt Brace Jovanovich, 1971.

KERPELMAN, L. C. "Student Political Activism and Ideology: Comparative Characteristics of Activists and Nonactivists." *Journal of Counseling Psychology,* 1969, *16.*

KERPELMAN, L. C. *Activists and Nonactivists: A Psychological Study of American College Students.* New York: Behavioral Publications, 1972.

KORTEN, F. F., COOK, S. W., AND LACEY, J. I. (Eds.) *Psychology and the Problems of Society.* Washington, D.C.: American Psychological Association, 1970.

LAUTER, P. Letter in *New York Review of Books,* Oct. 9, 1969.

LAUTER, P., AND ALEXANDER, A. Letter in *Antioch Review,* Fall 1969.

LIPSET, S. M. "Academia and Politics in America." In T. L. Mossiter (Ed.), *Imagination and Precision in the Social Sciences.* London: Faber and Faber, 1972.

LIPSET, S. M., AND SCHAFLANDER, G. *Passion and Politics: Student Activism in America.* Boston: Little, Brown, 1971.

Mayday, Mar. 3–10, 1969.

NICHOLS, D. C. (Ed.) *Perspectives on Campus Tensions: Papers Prepared for the Special Committee on Campus Tensions.* Washington, D.C.: American Council on Education, 1970.

O'BRIEN, J. "The Development of the New Left." *Annals of the American Academy of Political and Social Science,* May 1971, *395,* 15–25.

"Personality Test Provokes Debate." *Cornell Daily Sun,* Oct. 24, 1969.

PETERSON, R. E. *The Scope of Organized Student Protest in 1967–68.* Princeton, N.J.: Educational Testing Service, 1968a.

PETERSON, R. E. "The Student Left in American Higher Education." *Daedalus,* winter 1968b.

PETERSON, R. E., AND BILORUSKY, J. A. *May 1970: The Campus Aftermath of Cambodia and Kent State.* Berkeley, Calif.: Carnegie Commission on Higher Education, 1971.

RARICK, J. Quoted in *Congressional Record,* Apr. 20. 1970.

SCRANTON COMMISSION. *Report of the President's Commission on Campus Unrest.* Washington, D.C.: Government Printing Office, 1970.

"Student Protests: A Phenomenon for Behavioral Sciences Research." *Science,* July 5, 1968.

"Testing the Freshmen: ACE Wants to Learn How to Prevent Demonstrations." *Stanford Chaparral,* Sept. 25, 1969.

"There's a Man Going Around Doing Surveys. . . ." *New Left Notes,* Apr. 17, 1969.

WALLERSTEIN, I., AND STARR, P. (Eds.) *The University Crisis Reader,* Vol. 1: *The Liberal University under Attack.* New York: Random House, 1971.

WALSH, J. "ACE Study on Campus Unrest: Questions for Behavioral Scientists." *Science,* July 11, 1969, 157–160.

WILKINS, R. "The Case against Separatism: 'Black Jim Crow.' " *Newsweek,* Feb. 10, 1969, p. 57.

INDEX